MOHAMMAD
MY
MOTHER
&
ME

BENOIT COHEN

MOHAMMAD MY MOTHER & ME

TRANSLATED FROM THE FRENCH BY MICHELLE NOTEBOOM

POINTED LEAF PRESS

For my mother

"Perhaps you vaguely feel your fate is tied to that of others, that misfortune and happiness are two secret societies, so secret that you belong to them without knowing it, and somewhere inside there's an inaudible voice saying: As long as poverty exists, you're not rich; as long as despair exists, you're not happy; as long as prisons exist, you're not free."
—Chris Marker

PROLOGUE

My mother is waiting for Mohammad.

Who?

Mohammad, the refugee who's going to live with her. She repeats his name. Mohammad.

The refugee who's going to live with her?

She thought she'd mentioned it.

No, I would have remembered.

She put in an application with an association last month. They contacted her yesterday. She met him this afternoon in a Parisian café. She found him charming.

Why didn't she say anything?

I may live across the Atlantic, but I still would have liked her to talk to me before making a decision like this.

Did she tell my brothers?

No. It was obvious. It wasn't something she wanted to discuss; it was something she had to do.

I call Thomas.

"She's completely nuts. She's been talking about it for a while, but I never thought she'd actually go through with it."

"What's he like? Have you met him?"

"Not yet, but she already asked me to take him to a concert next week."

I chuckle. My brother lives a block from our mother. Whenever she needs someone to take care of her adoptive son, he'll be first on the list.

"You'll have to move."

"Unless she changes her mind. I wouldn't put it past her."

I call Julien.

"I just heard the news."

"Mother Teresa strikes again. Where's he from?"

"Afghanistan."

"It's going to be a shocker for him to wake up in a *hôtel particulier* next to the Eiffel Tower."

"What's the next step?"

"She'll probably marry him so he can get a visa, then leave him the country house in her will. *You kids are spoiled enough*," my brother snorts over the phone.

"We're such pricks."

"Yeah, we really are."

I heard it all. Grabbing women by the pussy. I read it all. Mexicans are thieves and rapists. I took it all in. Muslims should be banned from entering the country. I analyzed it all. Read every single survey. Got iPhone alerts every two hours to stay on top of the latest trends. I saw it all: Debates where an orange businessman called his opponent *a nasty woman;* rallies where he mocked a disabled journalist; the Ku Klux Klan urging followers to vote for a candidate they finally deemed respectable; hundreds of hours of political programs on CNN where everyone agreed he was incompetent, dangerous, and had no chance of winning. And then, the evening before the election, I listened, rapt, as Bill, Michelle, Barack, and Hillary spoke in succession on stage in Philadelphia. A mass display of intelligence, political clarity, kindness, generosity, and hope. It felt like nothing could stop us now, we were going to win. *We* being progressives, humanists, and liberals. I'd left the Old Continent behind for a burgeoning country where, after an African American, a woman was about to be elected President of the United States.

D-Day. The first numbers are encouraging. Voter participation is high. Experts are emphatic: the more people come out and vote, the better it is for Democrats. 94% of polls predict Hillary will win. And though the FBI's revelations slightly narrowed the gap between the two candidates in the final days, all systems appear to be a go.

We head out to spend election night at a party hosted by a French friend, a wine dealer from the south of France whose office is located at 724 Fifth Avenue, across from Trump Tower. I'm dreaming of a landslide, of reemerging triumphant later that night right under the noses of the billionaire's supporters.

We hop on the subway for Manhattan. It's 6:30 p.m.; the first results should be in soon. I try to check online. No connection in the tunnel beneath the East River. Why am I so nervous? Everyone agrees it's a done deal, there's no way she can lose. I put my hand to my mouth, but all my nails have been bitten away. I'm anxious for America, obviously, and for the world; but also, for us: Eleonore, the children and me. Two years back we decided to move to New York to live our American Dream, a notion that's clearly a cliche but, to us, made perfect sense. In Brooklyn, we discovered a new way of thinking, a new lifestyle, a permanent mix of skin colors, religions, fantasies, everyday solidarity, and infectious optimism. Living here is exhilarating; there's a joy and energy that makes life easier despite social inequalities. And today, that's precisely what's at stake.

We emerge from the subway on the corner of Sixth Avenue and 57th Street and find ourselves surrounded by Republican supporters, all headed to Fifth Avenue like ourselves. They proudly wield signs reading, *Thank you Jesus for making Donald Trump*, *At last a president with balls* or *Lock her up*. They sport *Make America Great Again* caps. We hasten away from the sickening crowd.

When we finally reach our friend's office, there's a radical shift in atmosphere. Everyone's speaking French. A huge television screen and about 30 plastic chairs are set up at one end of the room. The wine is already flowing freely, and trays of cheese preside over the buffet table. I quickly greet the other guests and take a seat in front of the screen.

The next three hours are torture as key states fall one after the other. The anchors from the various networks can't believe their eyes. They manage to maintain the suspense, but you can tell they're stunned. Meanwhile, the Frenchies drink red wine and eat camembert. Eleonore, me, and our Argentinian friend Fernando are the only ones aware of the unfolding disaster. We hear laughter over at the buffet. The situation is absurd. Finally, I can't stand it anymore—the news, and the guests' indifference, is simply too much. I suggest we leave and get up to thank our hostess. "What a shame you're leaving so soon," she chortles. "You won't be here to celebrate Hillary's win with us!"

"Are you blind? She's losing."

"Oh my! You're such a pessimist. So French!"

As we leave the building, we find ourselves amidst a sea of Trump supporters celebrating what looks more and more like a victory.

We walk through the crisp autumn night air in stunned silence. What are we going to do now? How can we live in this country anymore? For a few minutes, we entertain going back to France. Fernando brings us back to our senses.

"When you love a country, you can't just take the best it has to offer; you also have to fight when it's in danger," he states in his South American accent.

Stay and resist. Of course.

When we get home, I immediately turn on CNN. The gap continues to widen. The outcome is confirmed. Renowned commentator Van Jones comes on with a long face. *People have talked about a miracle. I'm hearing about a nightmare. It's hard to be a parent tonight for a lot of us. You tell your kids, 'Don't be a bully.' You tell your kids, 'Don't be a bigot.' You tell your kids, 'Do your homework and be prepared.' And then you have this outcome, and you have people putting children to bed tonight, and they're afraid of breakfast. They're afraid of 'how do I explain this to my children?'*

I'm paralyzed in front of the TV. I can't move. I see without seeing, hear without hearing. I think of the years that have passed. Thirty years of political life. I lived through the Mitterand generation, Pasqua's repression of student demonstrations, Chirac's retrograde right, Le Pen in the second round of presidential elections, Sarkozy and his bling-bling France. Then I moved here looking for something else: America, the land of immigrants, home of the Dream. And now it's turning into a nightmare.

My mother snuggles up under an alpaca wool blanket with a stack of magazines. She turns on the radio. Tonight, Finnish filmmaker Aki Kaurismäki is talking about his recent feature *Le Havre*. "Our treatment of migrants is criminal. I'm ashamed to be European. We've lost all our pride. There are more passports in the Mediterranean than fish."

She smiles sadly.

My mother is a beautiful seventy-year-old woman. Gorgeous wrinkles, long grey hair, and slender, time-worn hands. No hair dye, no face lift, no mounds of makeup: everything's natural. When she was younger, people would stop her in the street to ask for an autograph. They mistook her for Geraldine Chaplin. Of course, she was flattered. Once or twice, so as not to disappoint her fans, she'd sign the paper they handed her. Always elegant, never pretentious. Her only vanity is the tinted prescription glasses that have become her permanent trademark.

My mother's a fighter. She's buried four sisters, a father, a mother, and her husband who died one evening in September of 2010. They'd been married for 42 years, had dreamed together, traveled together, worked together. They were inseparable and complemented each other perfectly. When he passed, she did not pray. She believes in neither God nor heaven. She has never fantasized about seeing him again one day. She filled the void he left by making the most of a new kind of freedom. She started going to movies again, traveling places my father wasn't interested in, seeing friends who bored him, putting shallots in the vinaigrette, and blasting the radio. "My independence, which is my strength, implies solitude, which is my weakness," said Pier Paolo Pasolini. Today, she is free. Alone, too, in a house much too large for her. A vast 18th-century dwelling behind a Haussmannian building in the Invalides neighborhood of Paris. My parents bought it about ten years ago after selling their children's clothing brand, thus realizing my father's fantasy. He—a kid from a small village in Tunisia— had always dreamed of living in a bourgeois home in the center of Paris. My mother, however, never felt at ease. Too flashy, too pretentious, too ostentatious. I'll admit, I felt a bit uncomfortable myself the first time I set foot through the door. An antique stone stairway leading up three stories, enormous rooms, amazingly high ceilings, parquet floors that were hundreds of years old, tall windows overlooking a small garden, and multiple fireplaces. I was relieved I never had to invite my classmates here. After my father passed away, I pressured my mom to move and make a new start someplace else. Somewhere more in keeping with who she was. She wouldn't hear of it. She wanted to remain in the home they hadn't been able to enjoy long enough together. The house was *him*, and she refused to lose him a second time.

She turns down the radio and dials a number on her cell phone.

"Hello, Richard. Sorry to bother you, but Mohammad is not doing very well."

"What makes you say that?"

"We had dinner together. We made our usual small talk, then at one point, without warning, he told me he wanted to die."

"You know, refugees often have suicidal impulses, but like most people, they rarely go through with it. Given what they've endured, they're generally less afraid of death than us. They're a lot more resilient."

"Shall I send him anyway?"

"Tell him to drop by my office tomorrow afternoon."

"What about tonight? Can he sleep alone?"

"Don't worry, everything's going to be fine."

Mohammad sits at his desk writing in his spiral notebook, with a fountain pen.

Throughout his entire epic journey that led him to this room on the top floor of a *hôtel particulier* in the 7th *arrondissement* of Paris, he's always kept a journal.

I'm twenty years old, five-foot-five, and I want to die. I'm tired. Worn out by the burden that weighs on my heart and seems to get bigger each day. I don't want this life anymore. But I tried. I fought. I moved mountains. I always kept my spirits up. Oddly, now that I'm finally safe and settled, I no longer have the strength to carry on. I'm going to cut myself free from everything that causes me pain. I always knew it would be harder to live than to die. From now on, no one can harm me anymore. I don't care about anything. I won't have to worry anymore about the things that make life so hard. None of that will exist, because I won't exist anymore.

He stares into space. Out the window, rain falls, rooftops glisten, smoke rises from a chimney, and the Eiffel Tower looms against the dark sky.

Two days after the election, I fly to Paris. The trip had been planned a long time ago. I imagined returning triumphant. I go back with my tail between my legs. "So that's your tolerant and diverse America?"

At the airport, I buy a few newspapers and magazines. I grab a seat in a departure lounge and order a bourbon on the rocks to steady my nerves. The cover of the first magazine sets the tone: *America Died on November 8*. I move on to the *New Yorker* whose cover soberly depicts the torch of the Statue of Liberty, flame out and smoke rising from it. Inside, an editorial by David Remnick reads, *The election of Donald Trump to the Presidency is nothing less than a tragedy for the American republic, a tragedy for the Constitution, and a triumph for the forces, at home and abroad, of nativism, authoritarianism, misogyny and racism. Trump's shocking victory, his ascension to the Presidency, is a sickening event in the history of the United States and liberal democracy. On January 20, 2017, we will bid farewell to the first African-American President—a man of integrity, dignity and generous spirit—and witness the inauguration of a con who did little to spurn endorsement by forces of xenophobia and white supremacy. It is impossible to react to this moment with anything less than revulsion and profound anxiety.*

In another paper, humorist Amy Schumer is quoted: *Anyone saying 'pack your bags' is just as disgusting as anyone who voted for this racist, homophobic, openly disrespectful woman-abuser. Like the rest of us, I am grieving today. My heart is in a million pieces. My heart breaks for my niece and my friends who are pregnant, bringing children into the world right now. (...) I am furious.*

On the cover of another magazine, a huge digital clock reads *3 years, 11 months, 3 weeks, 3 days, 12 hours, 53 minutes and 58 seconds: Countdown until the next presidential election in 2020.*

I decide to go cold turkey. No CNN, no radio, no more *New York Times*. I toss the papers into the nearest trash and get ready to board. Before I switch off my phone, I take one last look at Facebook. Someone's posted a picture of Toni Morrison along with a quote: *This is precisely the time when artists go to work. There is no time for despair, no place for self-pity, no need for silence, no room for fear. We speak, we write, we do language. That is how civilizations heal.*

As usual, I pop a sleeping pill before takeoff, hoping it works the whole way until we land. The words of Toni Morrison continue to resonate in my mind. Of course, this is the time to go to work, to resist; each in his or her own way.

Paris. I get off the plane and hop in a cab.

The driver, a 50-year-old African, wants to chat.

"Where'd you fly in from?"

"New York."

"My condolences." He bursts into laughter. "We're next."

"You really think so?"

"People are fed up."

I'm too tired to get into it. I merely shrug. We're stuck in a traffic jam. I lean my head against the window and catch a few more z's.

I wake up an hour later on Avenue de la Motte-Picquet. My mother gives me a warm welcome. We sit in her kitchen where she's fixed me breakfast. Croissants, a baguette still hot from the bakery, and the raspberry jam she has such a knack for.

"You're moving back to Paris?"

She'd love that. But no, we're staying. I tell her what my neighbor in Brooklyn said just before I left. "America's always worked like that. Two steps forward, one step back, three steps forward, two steps back. But in the end, we progress." I cling to the image.

I decide it's the right time to tell my mother about the idea I had last night as I mulled over Toni Morrison's words.

"I'd like to write Mohammad's story and, subsequently, yours, as well. Explain how you met."

Her reply is curt. "That's of no interest whatsoever. Hundreds of thousands of people have gone through what he has, and I myself have no merit. With my big home and my means, I'm only doing what everyone wishes they could do. There's nothing extraordinary about it. I'm not heroic. I'm just nice."

I butter my bread in silence then give it another try. "Telling stories like yours as much as possible is what might finally wake people up to the fact there's a problem. And I don't agree with you; there's nothing trivial about what you've done. I know you don't like me to say it, but you've accomplished something remarkable. People need to hear about it, so they'll want to follow your example."

She sighs and pours boiling water into the teapot.

Out the window I spot Mohammad walking across the yard. I ask if he wants to join us for coffee.

He greets my mother with a kiss on each cheek. "Good morning, Marie-France."

We shake hands. The minute he sits down he grills me about the election. I tell him the whole story. He puts it into perspective. Another accident of history. He's seen plenty.

We speak English since he still struggles to hold a conversation in French. I take the plunge. "Mohammad, would you let me tell your story?"

"What for?"

"I'm not sure exactly. A book or a movie, maybe both. We'll see."

He studies me silently. I picture the information slowly churning through his head. What's he thinking? Is he flattered by my proposal? Or on the contrary, does he think I'm trying to take advantage of him? We barely know each other. We've only met briefly a couple times since he's been living here. I know nothing about him. Nor he about me. Why should he trust me? Was it a clumsy request? Too forward? Maybe he's simply reluctant to delve back into a past that I can only guess is chaotic.

After what feels like an eternity, he shrugs. I reassure him. "You don't have to give me an answer right now. We'll have a chance to talk about it later. I'm here for a few days."

I change the topic and talk about my daughter starting college. He's curious about the famous American campuses that students all over the world dream of. He, too, would love to go to college. Maybe one day.

As I'm leaving the kitchen, it hits me. "Why don't you come visit me in New York?" His eyes light up. "We could mix business with pleasure, spend a few days visiting the Big Apple, talking, take time to get to know each other better. Then we can decide whether or not to launch the project."

He smiles and promises to head straight to the U.S. Embassy the next day to get a visa.

• • •

New York. A childhood fantasy. All those American movies, sci-fi flicks, westerns, legendary boxing matches, junkie writers, jazz players, the music he listened to over and over, and, above all, rap.

Ever since he was little, Mohammad has loved music. Yet it was taboo in his family. He would listen in secret to cassettes of Afghan pop his friends lent him. He'd dance alone in his room. When the imams would recite their verses at the mosque, he'd keep time in his head. In terms of rhythm, the words and phrasing of the Koran are quite musical.

One day, a song by an Iranian rapper named Hichkas opened his eyes. From that moment on, it was all he lived for. He wrote, composed, sang, made videos. He was only 14. This lasted years. On the Internet, he discovered American hip-hop. At the time, New York was his Mecca. That's where the movement was born, in the heart of the Bronx. Mohammad was fascinated by street art, graffiti, breakdance, DJs, ghetto blasters, etc. He dressed like his idols with extra-large baggy pants, NBA T-shirts, and a cap turned backwards. He also developed a flair for fashion, concocting increasingly sophisticated outfits. His sole obsession: cross the Atlantic one day.

• • •

Back in Brooklyn, my cat Jalapeño has gone missing. A big Siberian tomcat with a Mexican name. Must've got scared.

Family crisis meeting. We print up flyers, search every empty lot in the neighborhood, and go door-to-door. The reception we get is amazing. The neighbors are extremely concerned. Some ask what brand of food he liked best so they can put it out to lure him; others offer to leave their gates cracked open in case he was out in the street;

everyone offers us something to drink to cheer us up. Losing a pot here is almost like losing a child. Then we talk politics. Everyone is in shock. Tim, a musician neighbor married to a Brazilian, shows me a video on his cell phone. It's the speech the Mayor of New York, Bill de Blasio gave before an audience of diverse origins. *Here is my promise to you as your mayor: we will use all the tools at our disposal to stand up for our people. If all Muslims are required to register, we will take legal action to block it. If the federal government wants our police officers to tear immigrant families apart, we will refuse to do it. If the federal government tries to deport law-abiding New Yorkers who have no representation, we will step in. If the Justice Department orders local police to resume 'stop and frisk,' we will not comply. We won't trade in policing for racial profiling. If there are threats to federal funding for Planned Parenthood of New York City, we will ensure women receive the healthcare they need. If Jews or Muslims or members of the LGBT community or any community are victimized and attacked, we will find their attackers, we will arrest them, we will prosecute them. This is New York. Nothing about who we are changed on Election Day. We are always New York. Somos siempre Nueva York.*

Like California, which clamored for independence, the State of New York plans to resist. There is every reason to be hopeful. Anything is possible. This is perhaps the only positive lesson in the whole election. Anything truly can happen here. The best as well as the worst.

When I get back from making the rounds of the neighborhood, I come up with an idea for a short story. I imagine a French couple who has just moved to Brooklyn and can't seem to make any friends. So, they use their missing cat as an excuse to meet people on their new block. Their neighbors show such kindness and concern that they decide to throw a small party to thank them. Once the wine is flowing freely and everyone's having a good time, the husband, three sheets to the wind, lifts his glass to propose a toast to his "new friends," then laughingly admits how they never actually had a cat. The guests are shocked and one by one make up excuses to leave.

Back when I lived in Paris, my mother and I would spend a lot of time together. Sometimes with the family, often just the two of us. We liked having lunch. I'd tell her about my new projects. She always had a strong, rather peremptory opinion, but generally offered good insight. I didn't necessarily listen to her advice, but I liked grappling with her vision of things.

Since my move, we talk regularly on the phone.

She picks up on the first ring.

"You want me to talk about Mohammad? I don't really have anything interesting to tell you. He's very secretive."

"Please, let me be the judge of what's interesting or not."

"You're right. Besides, I'd be delighted to spend time with you. How shall we do this?"

"Let's meet halfway."

Silence.

"I looked online. To truly be halfway between Paris and New York, we'd have to meet in Narsaq Kujalleq in southern Greenland. About 30 miles from Cape Farewell. At the last census, the population was 88. There's no airport or hotel. So instead, I'm prepared to make an effort. I propose Reykjavik. A five-hour-40-minute flight for me, and three-hours 45 for you."

"Love it. How cold is it in Iceland in December?"

"Fifteen degrees Fahrenheit."

"Sold!"

The first time we took a trip together was a year after my father passed away. I'd decided to take her to Italy. We'd spent countless family vacations there, enjoying *cantuccini* and *vino santo* at the Palio di Siena. Savoring grilled mozzarella on lemon leaves on the cliffs of Capri or *spaghetti alla bomba* on the shores of the limpid waters of the Gulf of Poets in our favorite restaurant on the peninsula. My great-grandparents had immigrated from Livorno to Tunis, and their love of Italy was handed down from one generation to the next. When my son, Aurelio, was five, and we asked what he wanted to be when he grew up, he'd always reply, "Italian."

My mother didn't feel she had it in her to return to a country so laden with memories; but in the end, she gave in. We got my father's car out of the garage, filled the tank, popped a Toto Cutugno CD in the stereo, put the convertible top down, then hit the road for San Remo under the blazing July sun.

We took a week to travel from Portofino to Positano on the way down, and from Naples to Lake Maggiore on the way up. Endless days making up for lost time, reliving our fondest memories, imagining a different future. At the time, neither of us had any idea I would soon fly off for other horizons. We reveled in the pleasure of each moment, interminable discussions in the family trattorias we loved so, with my father's ghost at our side.

A few years later, after I'd moved to the U.S., we repeated the experience in the southwest of France.

I'm already looking forward to our next adventure in Iceland.

Mohammad leaves the house, walks across the Esplanade des Invalides, crosses the Alexandre III bridge, and finds himself at the U.S. Embassy a few minutes later. The doors don't open for another hour, but there's already a long line outside the building.

He dreams about his arrival at the JFK airport, the nighttime skyline seen from the highway into Manhattan, the crowded restaurants of Chinatown, boat rides on the East River at the foot of the Statue of Liberty. And, also the things I told him about: the speakeasies of Brooklyn; the downtown theaters where you can lie back and sip cocktails while watching movies; the Bushwick murals; things that will remind him of his hip-hop years; and so on.

There are about 30 people ahead of him. A policeman comes out and announces the wait is at least three hours. Impossible. The tea room where he works as a waiter opens in one hour.

"What's your business today?"

"I need a visa. I've got a refugee travel document and have to visit a friend in New York."

"You need to make an appointment on the website for that sort of request."

On the way home, he phones the embassy to make sure he can get a visa without a passport. He follows the automated voice system, pressing this then that number, but no matter which option he chooses, a robotic voice always drones, "Consult our website." By the time he hangs up, he's already reached my mother's. He enters the gate, climbs the stairs four at a time, and sits down at his computer. His heart sinks. There it is in black-and-white: a travel document does not grant entry into the U.S. He doesn't get it; the civil servants at City Hall told him he could go anywhere with it. He slumps back in his chair, crushed.

He emails me to announce the bad news. I console him. We'll take a raincheck, promise. As soon as he gets his French nationality, we'll book the trip. New York will still be there. And I have no plans to move back to France.

I do some research on my end. He could potentially use his Afghan passport instead of his French travel document. After all, Obama is still in the Oval Office for a few more weeks. I google around and learn Afghanistan, along with Somalia, has access to the fewest countries in the world—a mere 25. In comparison, a French passport gets you into 175 countries without a visa.

Mohammad is depressed. He can't sleep. He feels humiliated. He knew he couldn't go back to his country—the lot of every political refugee—but he figured he could travel everywhere else. He called City Hall that afternoon. After an interminable wait, he finally managed to present his case. Quite bluntly, he was told that his travel document only lets him travel in Europe. For other countries, he needs a visa. How can he get one without a passport? Ask for French nationality. After two years on French soil, he's allowed to file an application. Then it takes 12 to 18 months for a reply.

He no longer feels like telling his story. He figured going to New York would free him from the emotional burden that has paralyzed him until now. Being halfway across the world in a romanticized, mythical city would have loosened his tongue. They say the energy in New York is crazy and makes you feel ten-feet tall. That's what he needs today. He's afraid of churning up memories he's kept buried for years. It's too big a risk. He's still too fragile. He needs to focus on the future and above all, not stir up ghosts from the past.

• • •

After his trip to New York gets canceled, Mohammad grows distant. I phone him several times that fall, to try to motivate him, but I can tell his enthusiasm is waning. I need to talk to him in person. I decide to book a flight to Paris. I can interview my mother while I'm there as well. Goodbye, Reykjavik.

Roissy. The sleeping pill trick worked. I'm raring to go. Mohammad and I are supposed to meet at 8 am that morning.

My mother is delighted to see me. "Maybe this project's a good thing after all."

The breakfast ritual. Earl Grey, multigrain bread, homemade raspberry jam and applesauce. I make small talk but can't help glancing at the clock over the stove. It's 8:15 am and still no sign of Mohammad.

"Did he tell you we were meeting this morning?"

"No, he didn't mention it."

"Ah."

I pull out my phone and dial his number. I hear ringing in the living room, then footsteps. It's him.

He kisses my mother and nods at me. "I'm sorry, but..." His voice trails off. "I'm a little late."

I breathe a sigh of relief, gulp down my tea, polish off my toast and stand up. My mother comes over and whispers, "Don't rush him, please."

Mohammad has told my mother very little about his past. She doesn't know exactly where he's from, or what he went through before stepping into her life. She immediately sensed a fracture in him, a deep-seated sorrow that really threw her. My mother is rational. Like a typical Aries, she rams forward head-first, dragging everyone in her wake. Her brother François compares her to Mick Jagger: a hundred ideas a minute, can't sit still, and shows no sign of weakness. She speaks her mind and looks head-on at the truth. With Mohammad, she has to rein herself in and adapt. She's gentle, attentive, and tries not to push him. She lets him make the first move. She knows it's a slow process, and everything is still very fragile.

Mohammad and I walk to the parking lot under the Place des Invalides. "Did you really come back especially for me?" he asks.

"Yes. For you and my mother."

"That's hard to believe."

"Really? Why?"

"It's been years since anyone's paid attention to me."

We reach my father's car, covered in a thick blanket of dust on the second underground level.

Traffic is tricky leaving Paris. We head for Recloses, a small village near Fontainebleau where our family home is located.

My plan is to spend the day by the fire with Mohammad in hopes he'll open up. For now, he's quiet. I fill the silence by talking about post-election America, people's anger, the daily demonstrations, the resistance taking shape; Obama, who in his last days as President, scrambles to do damage control before the tidal wave hits, and, finally, my cat that never came home. My monologue takes us all the way to the black wooden gate of our property.

I take the key hidden in the bushes to the left of the door and enter the house, a haven of serenity. My parents spent years fixing up every last detail of the place. Nothing could look new. One day during the renovation, when the floor of the second-story hallway collapsed, my father asked the mason to rebuild it exactly as before, and to make sure the terracotta floor tiles were damaged, irregular and uneven.

My father had a passion for creating and decorating new places. An apartment, a country home, a shop, anything at all, as long as it involved masonry, plumbing, woodworking or painting. He loved to spend evenings drafting meticulous plans down to the tiniest detail, just as much as installing a towel rack unearthed at an English flea market or a hook pre-rusted with a paintbrush to blend into a period decor. And when he'd find himself out of work due to lack of a personal project, he'd willingly offer his services to an uninspired friend or a not very handy cousin.

The people he most liked to spend time with were those who worked on his building projects. Michel, José, Manoel, his partners-in-crime, fellow travelers and friends, all in attendance the day of his cremation at Père-Lachaise cemetery. And when my mother, a few years after his death, decided to empty out his closets—filled with basically identical jackets, shirts and sweaters—she invited them to come help themselves. They took turns trying on clothes in the bathroom they themselves had painted, papered or tiled a few years earlier.

Since Mohammad has come to live at my mother's, she's often invited him for weekends at the country house by the forest. The first time was just two weeks after he'd arrived in Paris. They spent hours speaking intimately while my brother's children played in the garden. That was when Mohammad realized he could trust her.

As he's about to grant me this same trust, Mohammad seems nervous and shy. Is he going to turn on his heels and run? I offer to make tea to set him at ease.

"I need something stronger. Something to boost me up. Think there's any beer in the fridge?"

I smile. He justifies himself. "I haven't had alcohol in the morning for years."

I pull two armchairs over to the fireplace, wad up some newspaper, stack a few logs and strike a match. The kindling catches immediately. I fetch Mohammad a pale ale and make myself a cup of smoked black tea.

We sit facing each other. I take out my recorder, turn it on and set it on the coffee table between us.

He eyes me up and down. I smile. Mustn't rush him.

I know nothing about his story. I hope I won't be disappointed. I remember a documentary I shot a few years ago about a famous French writer. After two long days of interviews, I realized he was simply incapable of talking about himself or his work. Too self-conscious, and probably too humble. I had a choice: either I could continue the shoot, knowing perfectly well I'd never be able to make a movie out of it, or else cut my losses. I chose the latter. The author was angry, and we never saw each other again. What if this is the same? What if Mohammad's story turns out to be banal? What if my mother was right, and what he's been through has already been told before? What if I have to give up the project? How would I break the news without hurting him?

Mohammad sips the beer silently, his eyes glued to me. The fire crackles. Crows caw outside in the yard.

I take a deep breath. "Tell me your story from the beginning."

"The beginning…" He giggles nervously. "The very beginning?"

Mohammad is born.

This happens in 1994 in Iran. He's the seventh child and has three brothers and three sisters. His family is very religious. They are Shiite Muslims.

His father works in a textile mill and his mother looks after the children. They left Afghanistan in the late 1980s. The war with the Soviets was dragging on. They lived in Kabul and, at that time, the government was forcing every man of combat age into the army. Mohammad's father was called up, but he escaped. He didn't want to go to war; the conflict made no sense to him. He chose to flee the country before they caught him a second time.

They live in a large home in the suburbs of Isfahan. The house is very old and has no conveniences, but it's colorful and spacious. There's a large yard with high walls to protect the privacy of the women in the family. In the middle grows a splendid pomegranate tree.

Mohammad's father is a generous man and, despite his meager salary, regularly donates to different neighborhood organizations. He participates actively in the life of the Afghan community in the north of the city. There are always people at the house. Neighbors bring food as a sign of gratitude. Mohammad's family hosts many parties and banquets. Everyone bands together against the brutal discrimination they endure from the Iranian authorities.

One day, his father suffers an accident at the textile mill where he works. His right index finger is crushed in a weaving machine. Since he has no insurance or health care coverage, he must go back to work as soon as he's out of the hospital.

His parents are uneducated and unworldly. Mohammad always figured it was their fate to remain modest folk—with no future and no rights—to suffer through their lives. In that society, the thought of choosing your future is inconceivable. You can't have any ambition or think big. Developing a personality or being original is not an option. Everything is set up to prevent people from expressing any difference.

Mohammad stops to catch his breath, polishes off his beer and grins shyly. I encourage him to continue. He pauses, grabs a log from the wicker basket next to the fireplace and lays it on the fire.

Why has he agreed to talk to me? What is it about me that's inspired him to open up? Does he feel indepted to my mother? Is he simply touched by the fact I've shown an interest in him? Most of the relationships he has with the people he meets at my mother's are superficial. People are curious to see "Marie-France's migrant." He doesn't exist for them. In their eyes, he's just an exotic episode in my mother's life. That's the extent of it.

• • •

Starting from a young age, Mohammad is forced to pray with his parents, study religious texts, go to the mosque and be a good Muslim. He follows their precepts to the letter. He often asks God for forgiveness, even for sins he hasn't committed. He must shun any form of enjoyment or pleasure because his sole mission on earth is to worship Allah. Still, he can't help feeling happy, occasionally, for little things. A cat rubbing against his leg, the smell of a cake baking or the warm sun on his face. Consequently, he feels like he's living in constant sin. It makes him sad, and he chides himself for not being disciplined enough. To make up for it, he's very active at the mosque and participates in endless readings of the Koran in small groups. He also has to pray three times a day: at dawn, at noon and at night before bed. Every day. Without fail. The morning is the hardest, especially in the summer when the sun comes up at 5 am. Torture. When he's seven, he observes Ramadan for the first time. Another painful ordeal.

Mohammad quickly realizes if he wants to be accepted by his parents, brothers, sisters, friends of the family and his buddies, he must blend in. He must blindly follow religious practices without questioning. He gradually learns to eradicate any and all personal ambition, needs and desires. He grows increasingly frustrated but can't let it show. He has more and more questions but struggles not to answer them, so he won't go crazy. Do all the people around him who seem so faithful feel the same way? Are they merely pretending, too? Or is he the only one who is different?

My name is Cohen, therefore, I'm Jewish. Well, not really. My name is Cohen so I feel Jewish. My father was Jewish, my mother was not. And I'm not religious. So, I'm not considered Jewish by Jews. But I'm often considered Jewish by non-Jews. I feel a solidarity with Jewish people, but I don't support the politics of Israel. I feel close to the Jewish community: I like North African Jewish food; I appreciate Jewish music and Jewish traditions, but I rarely celebrate Jewish holidays.

For a long time, my only relationship to the religion was my grandmother's couscous for Yom Kippur. We would unfailingly gather in her old apartment on Place Pereire in the north of Paris. There was never any question of atonement or fasting, but it was an opportunity for us all—parents, brothers, aunts, uncle, cousins and grandparents—to get together. We were like those families who celebrate Christmas without ever saying a prayer. We would feast on *mechouia* salad, brik pastry with tuna, fine-grain semolina, and my grandmother's famous artichoke dumplings. For dessert: orange fruit salad and *deblah*, rosebud-shaped pastries drenched in orange-blossom syrup and honey. The evening ended in the living room, where my grandfather would smoke a cigar while we'd enjoy a Mars bar and a glass of Tropicana orange juice. I was a kid, and for me, that's what it meant to be Jewish.

J ust as he is starting to adjust to his new school, Mohammad has to leave his hometown. A serial killer is on the loose in the suburbs of Isfahan. Several women have been murdered in a single week. Inhabitants, convinced the killer is Afghan, start systematically chasing down, beating and slitting the throats of every Afghan they encounter.

Iranian society has never shown him the slightest esteem. Mohammad now knows for certain he could wind up stabbed in a ditch without any of them blinking an eye. The family flees in haste, leaving their home, belongings and friends behind.

The shadow of a doubt crosses my mind. This serial killer business sounds straight out of a movie. What if Mohammad is making up stories? What if he's afraid his life will come across as too dull, so he's spinning yarns and fabricating events? What if he's casting himself into a tale? I study his face for any sign of nervousness, but he carries on without batting an eye.

In Tehran, Mohammad and his family are taken in by distant cousins until they can find a place of their own. They sleep nine in one room. His father has a hard time finding work. Mohammad isn't allowed to go to school because he no longer has any textbooks or supplies. They were only able to each bring one small suitcase apiece. After a few months, they realize not a single school in the city accepts Afghan pupils. Volunteers in the neighborhood set up a makeshift classroom in a garage and take turns giving lessons.

They start over from scratch. Mohammad is nine, the youngest, and it's hardest for him. He starts to doubt the meaning of life, and, for the first time, he toys with the idea of suicide. Why should he have to pay for something he has no hand in? If there really is a God, how could He let such injustice exist? Once again, Mohammad must keep his thoughts to himself. Asking questions is not an option. He's surrounded by robots.

In Isfahan, the serial killer is finally caught. Turns out he wasn't Afghan but Iranian, from a good family to boot. But in the meantime, dozens of innocent people were killed, and hundreds of families, like Mohammad's, lost everything.

Mohammad needs some air. He gets up and steps outside. Out the window, I see him walking across the damp grass in the shade of the old oaks that surround the house. He lingers near a spot way off in the backyard where my mother planted some rose bushes. There's a sandstone boulder there marking where my father's ashes are buried. On the rock sits a small, Indian, sculpted wood chest where everyone can place a letter, drawing or object in his memory. One evening, unobserved, I slipped a note inside.

My father (1941-2010)
—Also known as Nono by his children or Captain Cook
  when he was at sea
—Loved my mother's spaghetti with tomato and basil
—Was crazy about soccer (had heart trouble in 2000
  when the French team scored a goal during the extra
  time thereby winning the European Championship)
—Played tennis left-handed
—Read the sports paper every morning
—Listened to jazz, salsa, and Italian pop music
—Was happiest with a hammer, screwdriver or
  paintbrush in his hand
—Knew every aisle of the hardware section in the local
  department store by heart, where the sales
  assistants all called him "Mister Cohen"
—Loved the feel of hot sand beneath his feet and the
  scent of jasmine
—Had an impressive collection of Brooks Brothers
  boxer shorts and wool socks all the same color
—Drove too fast with the wind in his hair
—Laughed a lot
—Hated growing old
—His last word : «Amazing»

Seeing him there near my father's grave, I realize just how much a part of the family Mohammad is becoming.

He stops and turns to look at the house. Our eyes meet. He nods and comes back in to resume his place in the armchair across from me.

"You know, I've never talked so much before."

I offer him another beer.

• • •

Every night after class, Mohammad works at a tailor's. He carries bolts of fabric and cleans the shop. In the meantime, his father gets a job in a textile mill, but the pay isn't enough to meet the family's needs.

Mohammad and his classmates stick together. They are all in the same boat. For the first time in his life, he has friends. He doesn't feel alone anymore.

On the other hand, outside the neighborhood, things are getting complicated. If he's standing in line at the market and an Iranian turns up, he cuts in front. If Mohammad dares look him in the eye, he gets shoved. If he dresses nicely, he is insulted or picked on. He has to make sure not to stand out. He has to be invisible, nonexistent. And if he is unlucky enough to somehow get mixed up in a fight, even if he has nothing to do with it, he immediately gets the blame. He witnesses two of his brothers get beat up for no reason. It's terrifying. He lives in constant fear. And it's even worse for females. Iranians do whatever they want to them. Afghan women and girls are often sexually assaulted, and the perpetrators never get punished. Boys also get raped. So, when Mohammad is just ten, his brothers teach him how to drink. They want to make sure he can hold his liquor, so he doesn't get abused.

His life has no value. Worse than a dog's. Those men can decide whether he lives or dies. They never call him by his first or last name, simply "The Afghan!" It's their favorite insult.

My father was born in La Goulette, Tunisia in 1941. Like most Tunisian Jews, he had to leave the country in the late 1950s during Independence. At the time, the Jewish community in Tunis, the majority of whom were on the French side, found themselves under threat. Insults, attacks, confiscations, and so on. He was 18 when he arrived in Paris on his own, leaving his family, sunshine, and carefree living far behind. He enrolled in the Beaux Arts and, for the first time, felt uprooted. His older brother was studying medicine and had no trouble getting a French nationality; whereas my father had to wait for 15 years.

His parents and little sister came to France shortly after. They opened a laundry and gathered the whole family in a small apartment on the Avenue de Choisy in the south of Paris.

My mother and father met a few years after that. They got married in 1968 and I arrived a year later, followed soon after by my two brothers, Julien and Thomas.

At that point, my father decided to cut ties with his country of birth. He shunned gatherings of "veterans," Friday night couscous dinners, Sunday belote card games, and he refused to cross back over the Mediterranean, despite my mother's insistence.

Time went by, and as my brothers and I grew older, we, too, started clamoring for a trip to our ancestors' land. My father finally gave in, and the five of us set off on a pilgrimmage in the early 1980s.

We stayed in a nice hotel in La Marsa outside Tunis, a few streets from the old Cohen family home. After a stroll beneath the bougainvillea of Sidi Bou Saïd, a tuna sandwich at Saf Saf and ice cream at Salem's— evoking memories from his childhood—we returned to our hotel. My brothers and I went to our room and my parents retired to theirs. They decided to leave the bay windows over the garden open to enjoy the scent of jasmine and the cool air. In the middle of the night, my mother was awoken by a warm hand on her thigh. She turned over and saw my father sound asleep. Then she noticed a stranger kneeling beside the bed. He lifted a finger to his lips urging her to be quiet and beckoned her to follow. Time seemed to stand still. As she snapped fully awake, she started to scream. The man vanished. My father woke up and she explained what happened. He stared at her incredulously.

"Are you sure it wasn't a dream?"

"Absolutely."

He climbed out of bed in his shorts, stepped out onto the terrace, and studied the garden going down to the sea. "There's no one out there. Go back to sleep."

He shut the bay window then crawled back into bed. She nestled close to him.

The next morning, my parents went to the reception desk and asked to speak to the manager. A bald man in his fifties invited them into his office. They told him what happened and that they planned to press charges. The manager explained that half the hotel had been rented by a Qatari sheikh, and that the man who'd snuck into their room was probably one of his bodyguards. He apologized profusely and strongly advised them not to go to the police. It would only cause more trouble. Then he told them to be sure to lock all the doors and windows of their villa. My mother was livid.

"If I'd been alone and that bastard had raped me, would your reaction be the same?"

"I'm truly sorry, Ma'am, but unfortunately there's nothing we can do."

The holy patriarchy.

Mohammad is 15. After several years in Tehran, he's finally found his way, realizing he must avoid as much contact with Iranians as possible. He enrolls in an Afghan school, works for an Afghan tailor, and has Afghan friends. They go to movies or play soccer together in the evenings. He has a sharp sense of humor and can make his friends laugh, which makes him popular.

His eldest sister can't stand Iran anymore and decides to go back to Afghanistan. She tries to convince the rest of the family to come along. Even though Kabul isn't the safest place—one war having replaced another—it's still their homeland. Their roots are there, their family is there, and they can have their own house. In Iran, they aren't allowed to drive, own property or work anywhere but in factories. Their father's lived there 25 years but has zero social status. The only proof of his existence is a resident card he must renew on a yearly basis at an exhorbitant cost; even that could be snatched away at any moment.

Mohammad's father thinks it over for several months then finally announces they're moving to Kabul. Some of Mohammad's brothers and sisters choose to stay in Iran, but he has no choice. He's too young to live on his own and can't bear the thought of being separated from his mother. He's torn between sadness over losing his friends, and relief at leaving a hostile country. He knows nothing about Afghanistan, but how could it be any worse?

● ● ●

Kabul has been ravaged by war. Its buildings are in ruins, its walls riddled with bullets and shrapnel. Terrible poverty. Bearded men and almost no women in the street. Mohammad is depressed.

People make fun of his Persian accent. He knows nothing of the country's culture, customs or traditions. He has none of the codes. He's considered a foreigner there, too. "Hey you, Iranian!"

Another dark spot is his family's economic situation. His father, who's just turned 60, is unable to find a job. He stays home while his sons earn money for the household. Everyone works for the same tailor.

Everything Mohammad learned and experienced in Iran serves no purpose. Once again, he has to start over from scratch, even less than scratch. The unhappiness, frustration and humiliation he suffered for years have robbed him of all self-confidence. That needs to change. He's in his own country and wants to be respected at last. He talks to his father, who explains that, unfortunately, it isn't as easy as just that: as a Hazara, that makes him a Shiite, a minority that suffers discrimination at the hands of the country's Sunni majority.

I go online. The Hazaras make up about 20% of Afghanistan's population. They have Asian ancestry, probably Mongolian, and speak *hazaragi*, a sort of Persian dialect. They are also found in Pakistan, Iran and Turkmenistan. They have been displaced by force, enslaved, and persecuted by other dominant groups. Their attachment to Shia Islam while surrounded by a Sunni majority has often forced them into exile, especially in the 1990s when the Taliban took power. At the time, they declared the Hazaras weren't real Muslims and needed to be exterminated, leading to numerous massacres. For about ten years, a law has granted them the same rights as other ethnic groups, giving them first time access to medical care, social services and education, like Pashtuns or Tadjiks. Though inequalities were still great. The Hazara have turned to politics to make their voice heard, focusing primarily on education; a lifeline in the long term.

Mohammad is deeply bothered by the idea of being considered a foreigner in his own country. When not in school or the fabrics shop, he spends his spare time lying on his bed doing nothing. The more he cuts himself off from the world, the more depressed he grows.

But the arrival of UN troops brings a ray of sunshine. Americans, Canadians, Europeans... This is his chance. Mohammad simply must find a way to work with them.

First step: speak their language. He tries enrolling in intensive French classes. Too expensive. English is more affordable, so he settles for that. Mohammad is extremely motivated. Learning a new language stimulates him and he makes fast progress. He can feel the world opening.

Mohammad and I have been speaking English all day. We each have our hesitations, approximations, grammar mistakes, missing vocabulary. We help each other out. When one of us can't find a word, the other comes to the rescue. We're on equal footing and over the course of the discussion, we begin to form a real bond.

Learning English was always a big deal in my family. I'd just turned eight when my mother sent me to England for the first time on a linguistic trip. One week in a family of strangers. I cried non-stop from the moment I left Paris until the plane touched back down in France. The next year, same story, but for two weeks of torture that time. And so on and so forth until I was 15. Instead of spending summer vacation with my friends, I went to work as a lifeguard in a hotel in southern Ireland. When I got there, the pool was under renovation. For the next two months, I ended up vacuuming floors and cleaning bathrooms. I shared an attic room with a cook who was drunk all the time. He would sadistically throw a bucket of freezing water in my face when he'd return from the pub in the middle of the night.

For years, I held it against my mother; but today I'm grateful she was so stubborn. Thanks to her efforts, I understand English perfectly and can speak fluently. Though I still get frustrated when I fail to express my ideas as accurately as in my native language. The lack of nuance makes me seem more slow-witted than I am. When you speak a foreign language, you aren't as sure of yourself; you're more vulnerable, duller, shier, more reserved. You become someone else.

Mohammad and I share this feeling.

In Afghanistan, he could make people laugh—girls, his family, friends. People appreciated his sense of humor. He would love to be funny again but fears he'll never recover the ease and finesse that let him be witty. For him, laughter comes hand in hand with happiness. When he laughs, and especially when he makes others laugh, he's happy.

Lunch break. I let him choose between a snack by the fire or a traditional French restaurant nearby. He chooses to eat in. We make a quick trip to the village to buy a fresh baguette, pâté, and pickles.

Back home, we sit down at the big kitchen table, break the baguette in half and make sandwiches. The country pâté is out of this world. No Cohen or Mohammad could resist it.

"It's better than any restaurant!"

I nod with my mouth full.

"Your mother's a delicious, simple cook. The first time we had lunch together, she put out a saucer with olive oil, salt, pepper and mystery spices in it. It was just amazing. I never dreamed oil could taste like that."

• • •

Mohammad learns from a friend that a position is available at the British embassy, with a good salary, too. He heads straight over. They ask for a resume, but he doesn't know what one is. His friend helps him write one up. Three lines. It works. He's hired.

At first, he's employed as a janitor, cleaning the kitchen, bathrooms and common areas. After two months, he gets promoted to dishwasher. A few weeks later, a supervisor realizes he speaks English and asks him to wait tables. He finds himself dealing with people who are completely different from anyone he's ever met. Europeans, diplomats, politicians and members of Afghan high society.

Mohammad makes friends with Naïm, a server at the cafeteria like himself. A cultivated, hardworking, intelligent young man. One day, his new friend pulls him aside. "Do you want to read a book?"

"I don't know. To be honest, I don't really read books."

"You should try. This one's easy, and it'll do you good."

Mohammad likes the idea. Naïm disappears into the locker room and comes back with the book. "Let's keep this to ourselves."

"You bet."

Think Yourself Successful: Tap into the Technology of Thought is a self-help book written by an Iranian doctor, Alireza Azmandian. After teaching in the most prestigious American universities, he returned to his homeland to share his theories with fellow Iranians.

It's 2 pm in the afternoon. Mohammad just finished his shift. He goes home, sets down his bag, lies on his bed and opens the book. He is hooked from the very first paragraph:

Human beings have so much hidden potential within them. Only a small fraction and tiny, incipient nuggets of this infinite treasure have been discovered. People have yet to discover the unlimited ability and power they possess. Whatever we think, we create; and whatever we desire, we achieve. In such a world, no obstacles exist. It is a world filled with opportunities, and each opportunity can be turned into a source of wealth. Wealth is not limited to money; rather, all our positive achievements can be considered wealth. Knowledge is a kind of wealth, as are love and happiness. Having strong relationships are aspects of wealth. A deep connection with the spiritual world is also considered wealth. In the new world that is created by the principles of the Technology of Thought, everything can be different.

Four hours later, Mohammad reaches the closing paragraph of the book: *I wish you a productive journey on earth. For the rest of our lives, which shall be long lifetimes of glory and health, we will remain deeply connected. Now move forward and continually think yourself successful.*

The book is like a Big Bang in Mohammad's mind. Each obvious fact is like a breakthrough. Nothing will ever be the same again.

Up until that point, Mohammad's life has been dependent on the world around him. But now he is embarking on a journey inside his own body and mind. He is unique. Anything he wants, he can strive for. The idea that life can be more than merely going through the motions day after day is revolutionary. He has a conscience, and that conscience is infinite; there is an unlimited field within him to be explored. He has the right to be happy, and he realizes even sadness can be comforting if he choses to analyze it rather than suffer from it. He is euphoric.

Everything that has been instilled in him, all his beliefs, are false. He's been lied to, by society, school and his own parents. His father always said that he'd been given something precious by *his* own father, which had in turn been handed down from his grandfather before: life. But their goal had never been to live that life, to give it meaning or question it. No, it was simply a matter of passing it on as it had been given. No more. Eat, sleep and pray. Be a good Muslim. And the supreme accomplishment at the end of it all was heaven.

After the excitement of discovery wears off, Mohammad is gripped by fear: the field of possibilities before him makes his head spin. How can this society be so simplistic and closed-minded? How can his family and friends live like sheep, without ever questioning anything? All the brutality he's suffered—that they've suffered—could have been avoided if people had been more enlightened. He's lived the first years of his life like a zombie. His awareness is like a resurrection. The book is the beginning of a new age. The time has come to think freely, express himself without holding back, and live fully.

He is 16. He has just been reborn.

We all have a book, movie, phrase or image that has changed our lives. For me, it's a quote. I've had it tacked over my desk for the last 20 years. *They didn't know it was impossible, so they did it.* Those words by Mark Twain have guided, inspired, and given me strength to move forward, no matter what obstacle stood in my way. Every time I embark on the crazy endeavor of making a new movie, I repeat that phrase to myself.

I call my mother to ask her about it.

"What's shaped me," she says, "isn't books or movies or beautiful quotes. It's the example of courageous lives filled with hope, intelligence and modest ambitions. I've also had the good fortune never to have lacked anything nor to have had too much. The books that transport me are never fiction. I like reality, even in its tragic dimension. The only book I've ever read twice in a row is Albert Camus' *The First Man.* And then there are those verses by Fernando Pessoa that I'd like engraved on my tombstone."

With a touch of the dramatic, she recites from memory:

> *When spring comes,*
> *if I'm already dead,*
> *the flowers will bloom just the same*
> *and the trees will be no less green than last spring.*
> *Reality doesn't need me.*
> *I feel great joy*
> *to think my death is of no importance.*
> *You may say Latin prayers over my coffin, if you like.*
> *You may dance and sing around it, if you like.*
> *I have no preferences for when I can no longer have*
> *preferences.*
> *What will be, when it will be, will be what it is.*

She pauses then adds, "I'll just be sad to know that you're all sad."

Mohammad's English gets better and better. He discovers the Internet, listens to more and more rap, starts dressing differently, changes his haircut, and his behavior. He develops a new personality.

He also decides to change his line of work. He takes initiative. Lots of people dream of having a well-paid and prestigious job at the British Embassy, like he does, but it offers no possibility whatsoever of promotion. Reading that book has rid him of his fears, given him strength and ambition. He is no longer apprehensive about the future and can't accept feeling humiliated anymore. He's had enough of that boss who treats him so harshly. He turns in his resignation.

He plans to wait a bit before looking for another job. He has a little money put aside and wants to enjoy his newfound freedom. He spends the next three days sleeping and exploring the city.

On the fourth day, in the morning, he gets a phone call from Barbara, an Italian woman he met at the embassy. "I've got a job for you."

"Why me?"

"The first time we met, you spoke French to me. Remember?"

"I thought you were French. All I said was, *'Bonjour, je m'appelle Mohammad.'* To be honest, that's basically the only thing I know."

"Want to learn?"

"You bet."

"Sodexo is looking for a security guard. It's well-paid and not too demanding. If you do a good job, you could easily climb the ladder."

Mohammad accepts without giving it a second thought.

To celebrate the good news, he buys some treats at the finest pastry shop in Kabul and goes home triumphant. He tells his parents he's going to work for the French. They are proud. When he tells them his salary, his brother and sister can hardly believe it.

The next day, he signs his contract with the multinational food services corporation.

He starts the following week. They give him suit pants and a jacket and station him outside a restaurant frequented by French soldiers from the nearby military base. His job is to verify their badges. No one can enter without his permission. The feeling of power is new to him. He likes it.

The base is located 30 miles from Kabul. Mohammad works 25 days in a row then has five days off. He sleeps on site and shares a room with four other employees. About 50 people work there: French, Italians, Pakistanis and Afghans. He gets along well with everyone except a few of his fellow Afghans. Though he is only 16 and a Hazara, he has a better position and higher salary than most of them. They are jealous. His roommates are illiterate, extremely religious Pashtuns. He goes along with the prayer ritual so as not to cause trouble. He is terrified of them. In a society where contact with women is kept to a strict minimum, teenagers like himself often get sexually molested by older men. Mohammad tries hard never to be alone in his room; he hangs out in the common areas as much as possible, reading *Think Yourself Successful* over and over. He also writes rap songs in secret.

One day, he confides his fears to Barbara, and she introduces him to Marc, the head cook, a burly man from the east of France who's worked for the army for years. Marc promises to stick up for Mohammad, and over the next few days, the two new friends go everywhere together. It takes the pressure off.

Mohammad's new state of mind sets him apart from the rest of his co-workers. He feels like a misfit. He's just discovered it's possible not to believe in God, to be an atheist, which not so long ago was unthinkable. It's a mortal sin to doubt Islam; people get killed for it. Even if the Koran says one must explore and open doors to find their path; in reality, it's impossible. Mohammad can't speak to the people around him. He feels alone.

He talks with the French soldiers every chance he gets. He asks them about their country, customs and beliefs. They seem to like him. One day, one of them suggests he come work with them as an interpreter. A dangerous job but well-paid, and a lot more exciting than checking badges outside a restaurant door. They are heading out on a mission to a war zone at the end of the month and need an answer quickly.

Going to the front, being an intermediary between the soldiers and villagers. Mohammad is tempted by the new adventure but isn't sure he wants to put his life at risk. He needs to think about it.

After a restless night, he decides to take the plunge. If he wants to get out of Afghanistan, working with foreign armies is an unhoped-for opportunity. *Inch'Allah*.

What he doesn't realize is that nobody comes out unscathed from the kind of experience he is about to embark upon.

In 1999, I shot a documentary on James Ellroy in Los Angeles. Two weeks alongside the *Mad Dog of American Crime Fiction*. Ellroy would peer straight into the camera and talk about his mother's murder when he was ten, his teenage years on drugs, his discovery of writing. After publishing a dozen crime novels, that made him a celebrity in the genre, he decided to hire Bill Stoner, a retired cop, to re-open the investigation into his mother's murder. It had been an unsolved case, filed away by the LAPD for years. I wanted to interview the former detective about his work with Ellroy. Stoner and I met at the Pacific Dining Car, a legendary steakhouse decorated like a railway train car. He talked about his time with the Los Angeles Police; time spent chasing the thieves, dealers, and killers of the City of Angels. And, how in the end, he started to enjoy it. I told him about my friend Eddie Bunker, LA novelist and former bank robber who appeared in my first movie, *Caméléone*. They must have crossed paths. Stoner confirmed he'd arrested Bunker several times. I assured him, jokingly, that Bunker was a great guy. The detective's face darkened. With a stony expression, he explained that bank robbers are not *great guys*. "Victims of hold-ups or hostage takings are permanently damaged. Their lives are fucked. It's like going to war or having a close brush with death. You never recover from it."

Mohammad asks for a break. He stands up and disappears down the hallway. I hear the bathroom door lock. My phone rings. It's my mother checking in. "Well?"

"It's going fine."

"It's not too rough for him?"

"On the contrary, I get the feeling he's actually relieved. He keeps thanking me."

"Has he said anything about me?"

"Not yet. We're taking our time. I gave him some beer, it's loosening him up."

"Careful, he can drink a lot."

"Then we were made for each other."

"That's not funny. What time will you be back?"

"When we're done."

It made me wonder, where was I at 16? I lived on the fourth floor of a bourgeois building in the center of Paris with my parents and two brothers. I'd just gotten expelled from a fancy private school for bad behavior. I toured around Europe with my buddies—Munich, Vienna, Budapest—but I cut the trip short to meet my girlfriend back in France. Her name was Nathalie, and I'd just lost my virginity to her. I'd often pick her up after high school and ride the subway to her stop. We'd kiss for a while, then she'd cross the footbridge over the ring road. I wasn't allowed to follow, and walking her home was out of the question. I later learned her father was anti-Semitic. I started going to the movies a lot. As a teenager, my idols were filmmakers Bergman, Tarkovsky and Kieslowski. Other than my grandmother, who died of cancer when I was nine, I'd never had any experience with death.

• • •

Overnight, Mohammad finds himself in a bulletproof vest on the front line. The soldiers around him fall like flies. It's terrifying. The conflict between the international coalition-backed Afghan government and the Taliban is ruthless.

He decides not to tell his parents the whole truth. It would make his mother sick. With his first paycheck, he buys them presents and gives them money. He tells them to eat their fill, treat themselves and not worry about anything. He suggests his father put part of Mohammad's earnings aside to save up for the land he's always dreamed of building a house on. One day, his mother sees some footage of French troops in action on TV. Bombs, death, blood.

"Is that your job?"

He downplays it. Says sometimes things get tense, but in general it's pretty calm. If only she knew! The ambushes, fear, violent fighting, constant nightmares, murdered civilians, legs blown off, the whistling of bullets, the stench of death. And that isn't the worst of it. The most revolting of all is the cynicism of the French army. Mohammad translates confidential information and gets the impression it's all just a game to them. A power struggle of anything goes. He'd been naïve to think they were there to protect the people. What a joke! They lie to the media, they lie to the government, they even lie to their own troops. In his oversized bulletproof vest, Mohammad has a front row seat where he helplessly witnesses the whole farce. He figures he'll wind up with a bullet in his head one day, either from a Taliban's AK-47 or a French soldier's FAMAS. With everything he knows, there's no way they'll ever let him go alive. He clings to an idea: as long as he's useful, he'll be safe. He tries not to think about the future.

Officially, the French, Americans, and 30 other nations are fighting the Taliban. The troops on the ground know who their enemy is. But the top-secret information Mohammad translates paints an entirely different picture. The truth is no one wants peace. The war suits them all. Everyone wants to sell their tanks and airplanes, justify the billions they pour into their armies, keep their factories busy, and distract their people.

The conversations he's privy to leave no doubt. Peace is not one of the objectives. They don't want to liberate the country; they want to control it. When he thinks about how President Bush invaded Iraq based on claims Saddam Hussein had weapons of mass destruction; and how he was re-elected a few years later, even though everyone knew he'd lied; Mohammad resigns himself to the sad conclusion that the only people who will pay the consequences of this ludicrous war are the Afghans.

All of that reinforces his belief that God does not exist. If He did, how could He let such things happen? Every day, Mohammad watches young soldiers, who believe they're fighting for freedom, get blown to bits before his eyes. And the people in charge never have to justify themselves. Every day, he loses a little more of his innocence.

Mohammad tells me that's when he became interested in political science. He tried to find books on the topic, but there were none to be found in Kabul then. The last major library in the city, with its collection of over 50,000 works, some dating back to the 10th century, had been completely destroyed by Taliban rocket launchers in the late 1990s. He turned to the Internet and read dozens of articles, watched videos, and visited the websites of the world's top political science schools: Harvard in the United States, Oxford in England, Sciences Po in France, etc. He secretly dreamed of attending one of the prestigious institutions some day.

One morning, Mohammad wakes at 7:30 am. He looks around groggily for his mother, then realizes he's at the base and pulls on his uniform. He crosses the courtyard to the refectory and sits on a bench to have a croissant and coffee. He looks around at all the soldiers and thinks of their families. Which of them will die today? Maybe it'll be his turn. Absurd. This is not his war. He feels neither French nor Afghan. What is he doing here?

He finishes breakfast and heads back to the tents. He has half-an-hour to kill before they set out for the front. Suddenly, he hears explosions in the distance. Probably French soldiers training their Afghan counterparts.

He lies down on his bunk and tries to relax, but the gunfire grows nearer and louder. He puts on his vest and heads to the camp entrance, stepping straight into a war zone. Dozens of bodies lie strewn across the ground in pools of blood. Mohammad ducks behind an armored vehicle. A soldier waves his gun at him, motioning for him to stay put. Some French soldiers were attacked while out jogging. No means of defense. A total massacre. Mohammad crouches behind the truck for several long minutes, listening as the gunfire grows more intense. He knows if the Taliban get into the camp, he'll be one of the first to get killed.

After an hour of intense fighting, the assailants flee. The soldiers tell Mohammad to go back to his tent and stay put until further notice. He lies down on his bunk, removes his vest, and bursts into tears.

He should stop there and turn in his resignation, but his family is counting on him. His father hasn't worked in a year, his brothers have moved out. Mohammad is now the household's sole breadwinner. He has no choice.

Every day, he leaves for the front with fear in his gut. He never talks about it, because more than anything, he doesn't want to alarm his folks. Nobody but them know about his new job. His friends still think he's waiting tables.

Most of the people he encounters, even if they aren't Taliban, hate the foreign troops. The television crews that come to the camp broadcast footage that make the French army look like liberators, but it is totally not true; the villagers hate the French soldiers. And that hatred is nothing compared to how much they loathe the interpreters, whom they consider traitors and collaborators. One day, a man tells Mohammad that what he's doing is worse than selling his mother's and sisters' bodies.

The army needs interpreters to communicate with the locals and the Afghan army. But the soldiers don't realize that some of Mohammad's colleagues are Islamic extremists, who now possess top secret information they can share as they like. Often, they say the exact opposite of what they are asked to translate. Mohammad sees it all but says nothing. He doesn't want trouble. He feels sorry for the French soldiers who have no idea how they are being deceived.

Mohammad has reached his saturation point. Despite the damp December cold, I suggest we take a walk in the woods. We cross the main street of the village and venture onto a sandy path through the bare trees. A half-hour of silent walking, then words begin to flow once more.

Ambushes, gunfire, street fighting, bombings, hostage taking, constant fear. After a year-and-a-half at the front, Mohammad marvels daily at the miracle of still being alive.

Then François Hollande is elected President of France and announces that, after 11 years on Afghan soil, French troops are going to be withdrawn. Overnight, Mohammad finds himself without a job. The soldiers summon him for questioning. Has he received any threats? They advise him not to stay in Afghanistan. Spies in the Afghan army with Taliban sympathies have gotten hold of the names of people who collaborated with coalition forces. They urge him to head straight to the French Embassy in Kabul the very next day, with his passport and every document he has proving he worked for them. There, he'll be given a visa so he can leave the country as soon as possible.

They insist. The Islamists are for sure going to take revenge on the interpreters. They'll be tortured for information then eliminated.

In a matter of days, the army is gone.

Mohammad heads to the embassy in hopes of quickly obtaining a visa. He thinks about his family and friends. He hasn't told them anything yet, but he hardly has a choice. He must leave. He values his life and doesn't want to put them at risk. It's the price for collaborating with the French army. Of course, no one warned him back when he was hired.

At the embassy, they ask for his passport and documents, and give him three months salary in exchange.

"You must stay in Kabul, and you mustn't take any other job, no matter what it is. Is that clear?"

"How long will it take to get my visa?"

"We don't know. There are lots of requests."

"The army told me to come see you because I'm in danger. Every day counts."

"We know."

On May 15, 2014, I turned in my application for a Green Card. A 400-page dossier outlining 25 years of my career in cinema, details about all my movies, 20 letters of recommendation, and a hundred some press clippings. Two weeks later, I received a positive response. There would be one final appointment a few months later to pick up the golden ticket. Everything started to accelerate: our family departure for New York; renting a house; enrolling in school; the move. The summer came and went and still no news from the consulate. Then school started. Jalapeño the cat joined our family, and the expiration date on our tourist visa was quickly approaching. In the end, we had to come back to France to wait for our appointment, which didn't get scheduled until three months later. Meanwhile, we lived at my mother's, had the kids do their school by correspondence, found a cat sitter, paid rent on our empty house in Brooklyn, and put our American life on hold.

On December 15, we headed to the American Embassy. After the routine checks, we sat down in the waiting room, a vast space surrounded by 30 counters where immigration officers would come and go. The numbers scrolled past on the monitors in the four corners of the room. The person we were about to see had the power to decide whether we would live on American soil. We were not supposed to be settled in New York already. We were supposed to wait for the official green-light before renting a house, moving, and enrolling our kids in school. We didn't want to lie, but we couldn't exactly tell the truth either. We'd rehearsed it a few times with the kids before the Big Day. Philomene, true to her 16-year-old self, was a compulsive liar, yet had lots of trouble with this.

"If they ask why you speak English so well, what will you say?"

"My grandma has spoken English to me since I was just a little girl."

"What are you talking about? I told you not to lie. For chrissakes, it's not that hard!"

"Right. Sorry."

It wasn't over yet.

After an hour's wait, our number flashed up on the screen. I stood up, took a deep breath and headed to window number 10, my lucky number, with Eleonore and the kids in tow. It was a female officer. She asked us, in French, to introduce ourselves one-by-one. She spent the next ten minutes grilling me, mainly about my movies; in particular, the last one that won a bunch of awards in American festivals and made it possible for us to apply directly for a Green Card. I tell her how Aurelio played the lead role in the feature-length film and Eleonore played his mother. A family affair. She smiled. She asked what we planned to do in the U.S., spent a long time looking at her computer, then studied us for a few seconds.

"I'm going to grant the visa to the three of you, but not him," she said, pointing at Aurelio.

My blood froze. How could we go without him? We'd already paid tuition, rented out our condo in Paris, shipped off a container with our things, adopted an American cat... Now what? One of us could go with Philomene, so she could at least finish her first year of school, while the other one stayed in Paris with Aurelio? Ridiculous!

I looked up. "Why?"

"He's going to break too many hearts in the U.S."

Eleonore and I exchanged a nervous smile.

"Congratulations!"

We thanked her politely. I removed my hands from the counter leaving two puddles of sweat.

We waited until we got outside the embassy then whooped with joy.

Three months later, still no news from the embassy. Mohammad keeps a low profile, triple locks his doors, and stops answering his phone. He rents a studio in downtown Kabul to wait for the visa. He doesn't want to endanger his folks. To pass the time, he listens to rap music. He tries to write new songs but can't focus. He'll make music again once he's safe.

Through social media he learns some of his fellow interpreters have already left the country, living in various cities in France. He returns to the embassy to find out what's going on. The situation is unbearable, he's in danger and can't go on like this. They say his application is under consideration. Mohammad insists. The man at the counter raises his voice and tells him to "stop being such a pain in the ass." What a world of difference between how the French treated him when he worked for them and now.

He has no money left to buy food or pay rent. Despite what they told him at the embassy, he needs to find a job. He starts handing his resume out around Kabul. Since he knows no one will hire him if his only job experience is at the tailor's, he decides to include the work with the French army, even if it's dangerous. He starts getting strange phone calls where people ask extremely personal questions that have nothing to do with the job he applied for. The callers hang up when he asks what's going on. Every time he goes for a job interview, he worries it might be a trap. In a stroke of luck, he lands a job waiting tables at the restaurant in the Australian Embassy. He gets a new phone number and changes the locks.

His days are monotonous and his nights, harrowing. He takes the bus early each morning for the embassy, making sure he isn't being followed. He spends all day in the restaurant, then makes the reverse trip home in the evening to barricade himself inside his apartment. He spends less and less time with his family.

The only person he sees is his best friend, Rohullah, whom Mohammad met back when he got into rap music. At the time, Rohullah worked in a camera and music store, and introduced Mohammad to his favorite groups and singers. Mohammad deeply admired Rohullah, a teenager from a poor family in the suburbs of Kabul who ran a popular shop in the center of town all by himself. Back then, they'd spend their evenings listening to music and dreaming of a better future. Now, as Mohammad is about to leave for Europe, Rohullah has just been hired as financial manager of the biggest university in town.

On February 9, there's a knock at his door. Mohammad isn't expecting anybody. Rohullah always sends a text or phones before dropping by.

"Who is it?"

"Package for you," grunts a man's voice with a thick Pashtun accent.

Mohammad freezes and stares at the floor, not sure what to do. The "delivery man" starts pounding on the door. Mohammad is absolutely sure they've come to slit his throat. He grabs his backpack in a panic, stuffs a few things in it along with his computer, then climbs up on a chair. He opens the window that leads onto a terrace and hoists himself outside. He crawls across the rooftop, leaps down to the street, and sprints off without looking back. He ducks into a mosque and sits on a prayer rug to catch his breath. An elderly imam shuffles over to say he is about to close. Mohammad explains how his life is in danger and he can't go back outside. The imam agrees to let him stay in the prayer room just this once, even though it is strictly against the rules. Mohammad has to promise not to make any noise. Mohammad thanks the imam profusely, then the man leaves, locking him inside.

The next day Mohammad returns to the French Embassy. He tells them about the assassination attempt he escaped and insists he be given a visa immediately. Despite his explanations, the civil servant asks him the same questions as the first time he came seven months ago. Mohammad loses his temper and demands to speak to the ambassador. The people at the embassy merely laugh in his face, and when he asks for his passport back, they throw him out. What is he supposed to do? He can't go back home or to work. Mohammad wanders through the streets of Kabul trying to come up with a plan. He's run out of options; he must leave as soon as possible. He goes to an Internet café and checks the list of where the United Nations High Commissioner for Refugees has offices. The nearest agency is in

Pakistan, a predominantly Sunni country—too dangerous for a Shiite like himself. There's one in Turkey but the wait is several years. The only office where requests are treated in a reasonable amount of time is in Sri Lanka. And you need a visa to go there. But to get a visa, you need a passport. Mohammad contacts a police friend of Rohullah's and, for a huge bribe, gets a new set of papers in record time. In Afghanistan, one of the most corrupt nations in the world, you can get anything for a price. Credit cards, fake papers, real weapons, soft drugs, hard drugs, stolen diamonds, police uniforms, explosives, expired medication, works of art, human organs, porn films, oil, uranium, ivory, and Viagra.

With his brand-new passport in hand, Mohammad heads straight to the Sri Lankan Embassy where he is immediately given a visa, then buys himself a one-way ticket on the next flight to Colombo.

With papers in order and a ticket in his pocket, Mohammad stops by to bid his mother farewell.

"Mom, I'm leaving. I don't know how long I'll be gone or when I'll be able to come back or even if I'll ever see you again, but I love you."

They fall into each other's arms and weep. Often when Mohammad was feeling blue, he'd go see his mother in the kitchen. "Come on Mom, let's go for a walk." He loved those times. She was his only friend, and he adored her. She was gentle, funny, and beautiful. As they say their goodbyes, he is flooded with memories: the smell of henna in her hair; the scent of rose on her skin; the soft feel of her cashmere shawl; the taste of meat pies she'd make especially for him; the cool sensation of *dogh*, a refreshing yogurt and mint drink she would serve in summers beneath the pomegranate tree; and, finally, the bus trip from Tehran to Kabul where they nestled together on the back seat, a moment he wished could have lasted forever.

"It's going to be a long trip, Mom, but that's life."

His father comes in. He is angry and doesn't want Mohammad to go. Can't he just hide out until the Taliban forget about him? Mohammad explains that they've already killed many of his former colleagues. He certainly doesn't intend to be next.

"What are you going to do? Where will you find money?"

"Don't worry, Dad, I'll figure it out."
"May God protect you, oon."

On the way to the airport, he stares out the window at the houses streaming past, the men, women, children, stray dogs, mulberry trees, willows and poplars. He silently bids farewell to the world he would most likely never see again. He doesn't care about Afghanistan, but he's devastated to leave his family and Rohullah behind.

I want to know more, delve deeper, ask for details about his relationship with his mother. Where'd their special connection come from? Is he so close to her because he's the youngest? How come he talks so little about his father? I hesitate. I don't want to put him on the defensive. I can tell he's in a comfortable space. As I weigh out pros and cons, he gets a jump on me.
"What was it like for you when you left your hometown?"

Even if it was a choice, I remember feeling like I'd betrayed my loved ones; like I'd blurted out, "I don't need you anymore so I'm taking off." Obviously, it's a lot more complicated, but it's still hard not to feel guilty.
For us, it was the day after our appointment at the consulate. We hopped on the first flight to New York. After 45 years in Paris, I was excited to discover a new world, meet different people, and have new professional experiences. The months we'd spent there, before our forced return, had shown us the exhilarating potential of Brooklyn and made us sure we'd made the right choice. I had no regrets about saying goodbye to my native city. Just a pang of emotion at leaving the people I loved behind.

The minute we got to our new home, I locked myself in my office to write my mother:

> *Dear Mom,*
> *Here we are in Brooklyn. What a change! So crazy!*
> *Eleonore and the kids told me how sad you*

were. I'm sad, too, of course. I'm torn between the joy and excitement of this amazing adventure, and the pain at being so far away from you.

Don't worry, we'll be seeing a lot of each other. You'll come visit soon, we'll be there for Christmas, and I have a film project in France next spring. It'll be more sporatic, but more intense.

We're inseparable.
I love you.
Benoit

She wrote back right away.

My dear Benoit,
Thank you for your tender words that touch me so.

I put on a good show, but when Eleonore came back for one last hug, I lost it.

Still, I'm so happy for you and your new adventure, so proud of how you handled this incredibly complex move.

I know your energy and ability to get things done, but once again, you impressed me!

Don't worry about me. New York is just next door (and luckily, I've got the means). It'll be a wealth of inspiration and a new place where I can enjoy visiting you.

Goodbye my inseparable son, see you soon.
Love,
Mom

Mohammad likes it when I talk about my mother. That was our deal. Give and take. He shares his story with me, and he can ask questions about my family whenever he wants. So far, he hasn't overdone it.

The day is drawing to a close. We still have so much to tell each other. Mohammad suggests we leave after dinner. He would have enjoyed spending the night, but he needs to be in Paris the next morning. He offers to whip up an Iranian meal. We arrive at the village grocery just as it's about to close and buy everything we need. At the checkout, he insists on paying. I let him. As soon as we're back at the house, he starts cooking. I fix us each a Hugo, a cocktail of elderflower syrup, lime juice and champagne, created by my buddy Dominique, bartender at the Rosebud, a historic bar in Montparnasse that's one of my haunts.

We raise our glasses in a toast. "To the future."

"This is the best drink I've had in a long time," he says.

Mohammad slices beef, peels carrots, chops tomatoes, boils red lentils, presses garlic, minces cilantro and measures out spices. I offer to help but he staunchly refuses. Tonight, I'm his guest. As he finishes dicing an onion, he turns to me clutching a long knife and peers straight into my eyes.

"It's just the two of us here, and right now, I could slit your throat in the name of Allah."

I stiffen.

"Yes, you could."

"See? That's why what your mother's done is so remarkable."

I fix us more drinks and turn the recorder back on.

At the airport, Mohammad heads straight for the departure gates. He has no luggage to check, since everything he's taking fits into his backpack. The officer at passport control frowns at him. "Destination?" he asks in a Pashtun accent. Bad omen.

"Colombo, Sri Lanka."

Mohammad shows the electronic visa he got from the embassy. The man tells him he needs a paper document and will have to go to the Ministry of Foreign Affairs to get one.

"My flight leaves in less than an hour. If I miss the plane, I lose my ticket."

The officer loses his temper and tells him to move on. Mohammad pulls out a bill, slips it across the counter and asks to speak to the airport manager. The man pockets the money and escorts Mohammad through the entire airport to a glass-enclosed office at the other end. He waves Mohammad into a seat and orders him to wait. The minutes tick by. Mohammad is going to miss his plane. His blood begins to boil.

Just as the loudspeaker announces a half-hour delay for the flight to Colombo, a pudgy, little man drenched in sweat steps into the office. He sits down across from Mohammad and eyes him scornfully.

"Where are you going?"

"Sri Lanka."

"What for?"

"To study."

"So, you're rich."

"No, I'm not. I've worked for years in a textile mill. I saved up."

The man's mouth curls into a smile, revealing a row of rotten teeth. Mohammad pulls his last two bills out of his wallet and places them on the desk.

"Please."

The loudspeaker announces the final call for flight UL217 with SriLankan Airlines.

"Please, sir."

The man pockets the money, calls someone in from next door and tells him to escort Mohammad to the gate. As they pass through the final metal detector, Mohammad's escort murmurs, "We know you have a stopover in Dubai. Our colleagues in the Emirates will take care of you."

He scribbles something in the back of Mohammad's passport then hands it to him. It's illegible.

"What's that?"

"Shut up, asshole."

Mohammad passes the final security gate and hurries out to the tarmac, forcing himself not to look back.

On January 27, 2014 at 11:45 pm, Mohammad flies off for the unknown with a heavy heart.

• • •

Same day. Same time.

My mother is propped up in bed against a mound of cushy pillows, half-listening to the radio while leafing through a magazine. Her friend Richard Rechtman, a psychiatrist and anthropologist specializing in the migrant question, is a guest on her favorite night show.

She sets down her magazine.

"You explain how, little by little, the asylum seeker, who was formerly accepted as a victim looking for freedom on French soil, land of exile, has been turned into someone undesirable, unacceptable, a person we suspect and ultimately reject," the host poses.

These are people who face danger in their own countries, and yet we turn them into a threat that must be eradicated. The Geneva Convention clearly states that any person who risks persecution or has suffered persecution has the right to asylum. So, this begs the question: how does someone prove they've been persecuted? Persecutors and torturers don't hand out certificates stating, 'I hereby declare that I duly tortured such-and-such.' There are no traces. And even physical evidence is questionable. Perhaps the asylum seeker was hurt as a child, maybe she broke a bone and didn't get proper treatment. How can we be sure this person is a victim of torture? So, we begin to think perhaps the best proof of persecution is psychological trauma. If the asylum seeker displays a psychotraumatic disorder, then he or she has indeed been persecuted, and we can be sure he or she is one of the good ones. See what I just said? The good ones. How revolting! As if there were good refugees and bad refugees. Those who can prove their suffering and the risks they took, and those who can't. But not everyone develops psychological trauma. Which doesn't mean the event didn't occur. The statistics are quite clear: only a third of people who experience a severely distressing event develop PTSD. That doesn't mean the other two thirds aren't traumatized. It just means they don't develop this sort of disorder. Currently, we restrict the conditions of asylum as much as possible in the name of something that's scandalous. We no longer defend asylum seekers, but asylum itself. It's become something so powerful that we have to make sure it's granted to those we deem deserving of it. The others then become illegal immigrants.

How are people selected?

What's awful is that the administration, which wields a great deal of power in this realm, asks the people who are the most ill-equipped for this sort of practice—volunteers, social workers, doctors, people helping refugees—to preselect cases, saying, 'No, that one will never get approved by the asylum authorities; this one may not turn out to have enough proof;' and so on. Instead of it weighing on society's conscience as it ought to, it's the people who work with migrants on a daily basis who bear the burden. And in the end, the figures don't change. They're extremely limited. The worst thing is that, in our democratic societies—as opposed to totalitarian ones—those doing the selecting are the people most opposed to the very principle of selection. We leave it up to them to suggest the just criteria for the injustice they denounce. It's tragic.

Tears stream down my mother's cheeks. Everything is a muddle in her mind. She recalls summer card games in Aveyron with my father; Mark, another psychiatrist friend; Richard; and me. Carefree days. She reaches for a Kleenex and blows her nose loudly. One of the privileges of being alone. How is it possible? How can someone decide there are two spots, ten spots, 100 spots, then suddenly stop? It's like watching two people drowning and choosing to save just one.

We sit at the big farm table in the kitchen. Chicken *soup e jo* to start, followed by beef stew, *Khoresh Gheymeh*. Mohammad is delighted to share the culture of his birth country with me. These are his two favorite dishes. He learned to cook as a boy back when he still lived in Iran. The main dish reminds him of weddings and funerals, where it's traditionally served. It's delicious.

"Next time, I'll make you butternut risotto with bacon and sage in Brooklyn."

We raise our glasses to this happy prospect, then he continues his tale.

He arrives in Colombo. It's hot and humid. Mohammad doesn't know a soul and doesn't speak a word of Sinhalese.

He'd tucked an envelope at the bottom of his backpack with the few hundred dollars he'd earned at the Australian Embassy. It's enough to live on for a couple months. He gets in a taxi and tells the driver to take him to the cheapest hotel in town, stressing the fact he is not a tourist. He winds up in a tiny, squalid, windowless room for a hundred dollars a month. Huge insects scuttle across the filthy floor. He has to share a bathroom with the other tenants, mainly Sri Lankan workers. The best rooms on the top floor are reserved for vacationers.

He heads straight to the United Nations office, shows his file, and is given an interview. They let him know that, as of that day, he is considered an asylum seeker, someone who has fled his home country, entered another country, and is waiting to be sent to a third country by the UN. Because he speaks English, he'll probably end up in Canada or the U.S. He would have preferred Australia, but they don't give him a choice. It depends on availability. Mohammad will have to get used to other people deciding his future.

He spends several months in Colombo waiting for news. As an asylum seeker, he's allowed to remain in the country but not work. Breaking this rule means immediate expulsion. Mohammad wouldn't dream of taking such a risk. Luckily, Romullah back in Kabul sends him enough money to hold out a few more weeks.

Mohammad is unbearably lonely. He passes the time drinking beer on the beach. One day, he meets two other Afghan asylum seekers, Jawad and Bagher, also waiting to hear from the UN. It's a godsend. They are Hazaras, like him, and Mohammad is thrilled to be able to speak his native tongue and share memories of his homeland.

They hang out day and night, laugh a lot, share their meals, and sleep on the beach under the stars.

After six months, as the excitement of their new friendship slowly succumbs to a dreary routine, the Sri Lankan government enters a conflict with the UN. Overnight, police begin arresting asylum seekers, throwing them in prison then deporting them. Mohammad and his buddies hastily leave the city to hide in Dehiwala, about a dozen miles away. The police gradually broaden their searches, keeping the three boys constantly on the move. They go from village to village, keeping the lowest profile possible. Whenever they spot a soldier or policeman, they cross the street, turn back or speed up. They seek refuge on deserted beaches and hide until dark. The weather's heating up and they're running out of cash. They barely eat, spending their last rupees on beer instead. Drinking brings comfort.

Mohammad has lost a lot of weight and is exhausted. It's a miracle they haven't been caught yet. They are living like outlaws, murderers even, whereas all they want is to save their own hides.

They are in constant fear of getting sent back to Afghanistan. Knowing they would first get routed through a detention center, a no-man's land with a horrible reputation.

I tell Mohammad that I was once in a detention center myself. His eyes narrow. "What do you mean by that?"

In the spring of 2009, scandalized by the way Sarkozy's government was treating illegal immigrants, I started writing a feature-length screenplay on the topic. For years, I'd been trying to get papers for Amparo, an Ecuadorian woman who worked at our home at the time. She'd lived in France for over 20 years but never managed to normalize her situation. Her fault: not having any children. She was part of our family, but we knew at any moment she could be stopped for a simple routine check, arrested, and sent halfway across the world. For over two decades, she lived with a sword of Damocles over her head.

My movie was called *The Alien Lady*. It was the story of an encounter between an undocumented Tunisian woman and a volunteer at the Cimade, an NGO that monitors the treatment of foreigners in detention centers and ensures their rights are respected. The two protagonists fall in love and decide to get married so she can have papers. The start of a long ordeal.

To lend my screenplay credibility, I got myself hired as an intern at the Cimade. Which is how I wound up in a detention center in Brittany.

When I arrived in Rennes on the morning train, Claire, one of the women from the association, picked me up at the station. We drove out of the city into the countryside to an ultra-modern building in the middle of nowhere. The new center had just been inaugurated, despite the resistance of several associations and a number of legal actions. The authorities decided to schedule its opening during the summer vacation so there would be fewer protesters. We parked in a large, empty parking lot, then walked up to the security booth. After our papers had been inspected and we'd passed through several security gates, we found ourselves inside. Even if regulations specified that the occupants should be called "retainees" rather than "detainees," it was obviously a prison. We walked through an inner courtyard, where a few men stood about idly, then into the refectory, a large neon-lit room with metal tables and benches bolted to the floor. All eyes turned to us. The tension was palpable. Claire had warned me that four migrants had just gone on a hunger strike, after a young pregnant Romanian woman passed out and lost her baby on the way to the hospital.

We skirted the tall mesh fence of the area, reserved for women and children, to reach the small offices of the Cimade. Claire would meet individually with the detainees to help them prepare their defense when they go before the judge.

Each undocumented immigrant that came through the office had a tragic story, only made worse by staying in detention.

"The people here live in permanent stress," Claire said. "They could be deported from one day to the next. And even if they are granted the right to stay in France, they're completely destitute by the time they get out of here. After one month in the center, they've lost their apartments because they haven't paid rent, they've lost their jobs since their bosses have replaced them, and they wind up in the street."

That afternoon, we accompanied a Nigerian man to court.

After waiting forever in a corridor with no windows, where court-appointed lawyers and their clients kept filing past, the man's turn came before the judge.

"I'm disgusted with myself. I have no prospects. And back home, it's even worse. People are starving to death. Some families can only eat every other day. Today, the parents; tomorrow, the kids. I left everything behind when I came here. Going back would mean losing everything again. Or else losing the only thing I have remaining. Hope. Sheer hope is what gets me through each day. If you take that away from me, it's over. You know, Mr. Judge, in my country we say that you are big because we are down on our knees. Here I stand before you on my knees begging you not to send me back."

"That's all quite moving," the prosecuter replied. "Mr. N. has a real way with words, which incidentally makes us wonder if what he says about coming from a village where people are dying from hunger is actually true. But I digress. Mr. N. entered France illegally and worked here with false documents which amounts to..."

I turned to Claire, staring at the floor with her hands clamped over her ears.

When I got back to Paris, I wrote an article entitled, "We're all Human Beings," published a few days later in *Libération*, one of France's most important newspapers. The piece ended with a quote from beloved actress Jeanne Moreau: *As a French citizen, attached more than ever to liberty, equality and fraternity, it is my duty to remind you, Mr. Minister, that you do not have the right to life and death over men, women and children who work, live and study here in France, a country that is disgraced today.*

The following day, I was astonished to get a voice message from the Ministry of Immigration ordering me to phone them immediately. I was to explain how I managed to enter the center. Big Brother was watching.

In the end, the project never got off the ground. Another filmmaker had tackled the same subject and swiftly made a powerful, successful film that sparked controversy and opened debate. A few months later, a deputy put forth a bill to decriminalize the *offense of solidarity*, in other words, aiding illegal immigrants. In the end, however, it was rejected by the Senate.

The stars are out. It's cold. We bundle up in our coats and sit on lawn chairs out in the yard. I open a worn leather case and take out two Havanas. Mohammad's a smoker, though admits he's never tried a cigar. From the first puff, I can tell he likes it. He closes his eyes and lets the thick smoke waft from his mouth.

"A new world."

After weeks of playing cat and mouse with the police, Mohammad, Jawad, and Bagher learn the government has struck an agreement with the United Nations, and they return to Colombo.

Mohammad still hasn't heard any news about his asylum request, and he starts checking out other options. Online, he discovers that Switzerland is the only country in the world to offer a humanitarian visa. That same day, he heads to the Swiss Embassy.

"Can I talk to someone in charge of immigration?"

"What's your problem?"

"I need a visa."

"On what basis? You're not even Sri Lankan."

"I want to ask for a humanitarian visa."

The receptionist asks him to wait in the lobby. She disappears for a few minutes, then comes back with a form to fill out.

A week goes by before he can meet with an officer to present his case. Finally, someone is going to listen to him. The man is shocked the French army left him to his own fate. He offers to go to their embassy himself to defend Mohammad's case.

"I don't want to go to France."

"Really? Why not? It's the country of human rights."

"I read on the Internet that it's harder and harder to get refugee status there."

"If I manage to get you an appointment, I would suggest you grab the chance."

Two days later, the officer phones to give Mohammad the personal number of a deputy advisor at the French Embassy. Mohammad calls him right away. The diplomat tells him to come the next day and urges him not to leave home until then, little realizing Mohammad sleeps on the beach.

The next day, he meets with Marc Lamy, a tall man in his fifties with short hair wearing a suit, who listens patiently to Mohammad's story.

"Do you know anyone in France who could put you up?"

"Yes, a cook who worked for the French army in Kabul. His name's Marc, like you, and he lives in Sarrebourg, Lorraine. We've kept in touch."

"Very well. I promise I'll take care of this."

"Sir, with all due respect, I've heard that so many times before. This time, I'm begging you; please do something for me."

"I won't let you down. You have my word."

He points out that if he does manage to get a visa, Mohammad will have to pay for his own plane ticket.

Before he goes, Lamy hands Mohammad his card, writing on it, *If you arrest this person, call this number*. He also gives him two T-shirts with the embassy insignia. "With these, you'll look more like a tourist."

Mohammad heads to the nearest Internet café and calls Rohullah in Kabul. He announces the big news: The French are finally going to do something for him! He's almost there but still needs his friend's help: $385 for a one-way ticket to Paris. Without a second thought, Rohullah offers to sell his laptop to pay for the ticket. Mohammad feels guilty. Rohullah is now working in a graphic design agency and uses his computer daily. But there is no one else he can turn to for the money, so Mohammad finally accepts.

Two weeks go by. Mohammad, Jawad, and Bagher stay put and hide on the beach. They only venture out after dark to make sure they don't run into trouble.

Mohammad keeps phoning the embassy. The deputy still hasn't heard from Paris but tells him to be ready. "If we don't get a green light by the end of the week, it means they didn't take the request into account. Unfortunately, it's out of my hands now."

On Friday morning, Mohammad receives a text. *Come at 11. I have your visa.*

Mohammad plops down in the sand and weeps. His two friends hug him.

The receptionist at the embassy tells him he needs to get his passport back from the UN so they can put the visa in it.

Mohammad makes a U-turn. Just as he reaches the avenue where the UN building is located, he spots two policemen coming toward him. He lowers his gaze and stares at his feet, trying to continue walking at a steady pace. How absurd it would be to get arrested now! The two cops are deep in discussion, and when they finally reach him, they walk right past without giving a second look. Mohammad breathes a sigh of relief and speeds up.

At the United Nations, they don't want to give his passport back. They have a procedure to follow. Mohammad will have to make an official request then wait for the reply before taking any other steps.

"You're useless. We came here thinking you were going to protect us. The police are arresting us, one by one, and you aren't doing anything to stop it."

"Sir, we've increased our meetings and appointments with the government to change things, but it's a slow process."

"And in the meantime, we keep getting sent to jail and deported. So please, just give me my passport back and let's call it quits. I won't ask for anything more."

The woman behind the counter tells him to wait and disappears into an office. Mohammad glances around. Not a thing has changed since the first day he set foot in this building, nearly a year ago. He's at the end of his rope. This is his last chance. If it fails, he'll probably lose his mind.

A half-hour goes by before the woman reappears. She walks up to him, smiling, and hands him his passport.

"I'm sorry. Good luck."

Mohammad takes off like a shot and races back to the embassy. Marc gives the passport to his assistant then peers at Mohammad. "Book a flight to Paris tonight. Don't wait."

"France finally kept its promise."

Marc sighs. Mohammad suddenly realizes he never heard back from his superiors and took the initiative to issue the visa himself, wanting to repair the betrayal and make up for an army that left men behind with a death sentence on their heads. Mohammad would like to grab hold of this guardian angel and hug him, but he settles for a smile of gratitude instead.

The assistant reappears with the passport then leaves again. Marc checks inside, then hands it to Mohammad along with four 50€ bills.

"Good luck," he grins.

Saying goodbye to Jawad and Bagher is heart-wrenching. The three have been together for four months straight. They've shared everything and helped each other unfalteringly. Together, they mustered the strength to carry on; clinging to the conviction that one day, they'd make it out of this hell together. So why Mohammad and not them? Their stories are exactly the same. They fled the same war, and certain death, and they, too, had lost everything. The injustice is terrible.

"We'll meet again on the other side."

They hug for a long time, then Mohammad walks away.

Mohammad heads straight to the airport, goes up to the Air France counter and buys a ticket. The flight boards in four hours. At customs, Mohammad is told that his visa for Sri Lanka has expired and his presence in the country is illegal. He can be put in jail and get sent back to Afghanistan. He's ordered to step aside and wait for the police. Uppercut. Knock out.

A lightbulb goes off. He pulls Marc's card from his pocket and asks the officer to call him.

"It's after midnight."

"He's a friend. He told me I could call him any time, day or night. Please, try."

The customs officer picks up the phone and dials the number. Mohammad can hear it ring. Once, twice, three times, four... Just as he's about to hang up, Marc answers. The officer apologizes for calling so late, explains the situation, and listens attentively to whatever Marc says. When he hangs up, his attitude changes radically. Everything is in order, and Mohammad is free to board his plane.

Mohammad goes to stand in the long line at the departure gate. A few minutes later, he spots the officer walking toward him. Mohammad's blood freezes. The officer strides right up to him and orders him to come along. Mohammad isn't sure what to do. The man grabs his arm and removes him from the line, then walks him straight up to the gate. The officer tells the guard outside the plane to give Mohammad priority. The guard lets Mohammad through without checking either his passport or his ticket. As he boards the plane, a flight attendant greets him with a broad smile. He sits down in 24A next to the window and shuts his eyes.

New plane. New destination. New hope. New life?

After a moment, the engines start to roar, and Mohammad feels the aircraft lift off the ground.

Atypical Wednesday. My mother is on her way home from Recloses, where she takes one of her grandaughters every week for a riding lesson. She drives her SmartCar through the city in the pouring rain. On the radio, a Republican candidate is going on about how if he is elected, he'll reduce the number of legal migrants. We need "minimal and tightly controlled immigration that responds to our economic needs and our capacity to take migrants in and integrate them." My mother changes the station.

She parks her car beneath the Invalides. As she emerges onto the esplanade, she spots a few dozen men gathered in the rain. They hold banners reading, *Justice for all; Solidarity for interpreters in danger; A visa or death*. As she walks past, she catches one of the demonstrators' eyes and smiles. He comes over and hands her a flyer.

"Hello. We're Afghans. We worked with the French army for years, we took the same risks as them. They're our brothers-in-arms, but today they've forgotten us. We here are the lucky ones who managed to get out, but a 100 of our former colleagues haven't been able to leave the country and are in danger. Just this week, two of them got their throats slit."

My mother listens as the rain drums down on her umbrella.

"To get a visa, you need to have worked five years for the French army, but the Taliban doesn't count the same way. If you could sign our online petition, it would help us."

"I will. Promise."

"Thank you, Ma'am. May God be with you."

She walks away from the small group encircled by an impressive number of riot police.

All this is happening to a backdrop of general indifference around the world. Yet for months, it's been the only thing anyone talks about on television, the radio, and social media: the migrant crisis. Syrians are in the headlines. The war in their homeland has driven them into mass exodus. They arrive at the gates of Europe, but no EU government wants to open their borders. We talk, debate, analyze, question and broadcast shocking images. The picture of a dead child on a Turkish beach goes viral and the world is outraged. People say it's a wake-up call that will unleash a mass movement of solidarity; but a few days later, some other picture has taken its place. The refugees with their struggles are forgotten. Meanwhile, we continue to welcome only a lucky few, while the others are left to die at sea, on the beaches or in the cold.

My mother walks carefully up the avenue, avoiding the puddles. She wonders what she can do on her own personal level to help lessen this injustice. She doesn't have enough time to get involved in a humanitarian organization; she's already making charitable donations to all sorts of NGOs; she always votes for candidates who seem the most apt to defend the idea of generosity for others she holds dear, but clearly, it isn't enough. What more can she do?

"We've begun our descent to Paris. Please return to your seat and fasten your seatbelt." The flight attendant's voice wakes Mohammad with a start. It's 7:30 am local time. Out the window, he sees fields of wheat, squares of green, patches of forest, villages with steeples, and tiny cars driving along country roads as if in slow motion. Everything looks so calm and peaceful. Then he spots the first buildings, warehouses, and highway ramps as they near the city. The Eiffel Tower appears through the mist. Down below: freedom. A new country to discover; a new chapter to write; an opportunity to exist; no longer be on the run in constant fear, a pariah, an illegal, a sub-human. The chance to be respected, at last.

The plane lands at Roissy Charles-de-Gaulle, and in no time, Mohammad is at customs. He gets in the foreign citizens line. He's impressed by the cleanliness of the airport. Everything is shiny and brand new. Even the customs officers look nice. Finally, it's his turn. He steps up to the counter and holds out his documents. The officer's face hardens at the sight of the Afghan passport. "Where'd you fly from?"

"Colombo."

"You're Afghan. To enter France, you must ask for a visa in your home country. How'd you get one in Sri Lanka?"

"It's a long story."

"Long stories are for my colleague in the office over there."

Mohammad can feel the other travelers staring at him. He avoids their gaze.

He sits in the dimly lit office for a whole hour before a customs officer finally appears. His friend Marc, the cook from the French army in Kabul, had come all the way from the East of France to meet him. He would be waiting outside.

"Why have you come here?"

Mohammad wants to scream, but takes a deep breath and coolly replies, "I've come to ask for political asylum. I'm not a tourist."

He pulls all his documents out of his backpack and spreads them on the table: the papers from the United Nations; proof of his collaboration with the French army; Marc Lamy's card with the embassy insignia. The civil servant gathers everything up and leaves the room. Mohammad hears a photocopier out in the hallway, then nothing. Another hour goes by with no sign of anyone. He calls out but nothing happens. His friend out in the arrival hall must be getting worried. The other passengers are all long gone, and there's no way of letting Marc know.

Finally, the customs officer returns. "Who do you know here?"

"A Frenchman I worked with on the base in Kabul. He made a special trip from Lorraine to pick me up. He's been waiting two hours and must wonder where I am. If you have other questions, please, ask me. I have a passport and a valid visa. I'm telling you the truth. What more do you want?"

The man glares at him, looks through the documents once more, as if he were seeing them for the first time, then lets Mohammad go without any explanation.

When Mohammad sees Marc, they leap into each other's arms. "A passenger warned me you'd been stopped at customs. I tried to do something, but they blew me off."

"I'm sorry."

"Don't worry. Considering how long we've waited for this."

"I did it!" Mohammad beams, and they hug again.

As they set off for Strasbourg, where Marc left his car, Mohammad can hardly believe his eyes. He's exhausted, confused, and fascinated by the modernity of the high-speed TGV train they're on. The landscape whizzes past at an incredible speed. Will his life move equally fast from now on?

"I'm going to the bar car. Want anything?"

"No, thanks."

"We'll have a drink to celebrate."

Marc buys two cans of beer and comes back to sit across from Mohammad. They make a toast. "You're safe now."

Mohammad nods, takes a few sips and drifts off to sleep. An hour later, he wakes up in the Strasbourg train station.

He's impressed by how beautiful the city is. Marc suggests they walk around a bit before hitting the road. They stroll along the canals and through the small medieval streets of the Petite France district, venturing all the way to the cathedral. Mohammad can't tear his eyes from a huge rose window featuring ears of wheat, and the multitude of sculptures ornamenting the massive façade.

"Have you ever had *choucroute*?"

"What's that?"

"An Alsacian specialty of fermented cabbage, potatoes and sausage."

"I can't eat anything. My stomach's in knots."

"Come on, you need to get something inside you."

They enter one of the timber-framed buildings on the square. Giddy from the warmth of the restaurant, the copious food, and endless steins of beer, Mohammad feels good for the first time in ages.

As they drive to Sarrebourg, Marc's town, Mohammad peers out at the countryside along the highway; but he's so tipsy and exhausted he can't focus on the scenery. His head is spinning, so he closes his eyes and leans his forehead against the window. The chill off it makes him feel better. Marc stops at a gas station to get him a coffee. Mohammad is amazed by the abundance of drinks, candy, sandwiches, ice cream, cookies and newspapers.

The following morning, Marc announces he's leaving in two days for a mission with a French Army detachment in North Africa. "We'll deal with your papers when I get back in a month."

The next 24 hours are spent exploring the small municipality of Moselle, surrounded by forests and ponds. Marc points out where to shop, explains a few things about his small, yet comfortable apartment, hands him 200€, and flies off to Algeria. Mohammad is on his own once again.

He buys groceries twice a week at the village supermarket. He communicates, as best he can, with the few words of French he learned from the soldiers. The people he comes in contact with make little effort to understand him, often looking at him askance. He even gets rebuffed by an impatient baker, who shoos him out of the bakery. The hostility is hard to bear. Mohammad stays inside as much as possible, sleeps a lot, and watches movies. Especially documentaries.

• • •

Mohammad and I both left our countries and live in a foreign land. I wanted a change of pace; he wanted to save himself. He had no other options; I did. I chose my adopted country; he did not. He had no money; I did. I felt at home right away; he did not.

The difference hangs on one word: Welcome.

If you don't feel welcome, it's impossible to integrate, find your place, and muster the strength to rebuild your life in a foreign country. The notion of 'welcome' is at the heart of successful integration. Trump's impending presidency was sending a dire message to the rest of the world. The United States, historic land of immigration, was turning insular.

The last time I flew back to New York, my biggest fear was having to wait in line forever at customs. "Purpose of your trip?" the immigration officer barked.

"I live here."

"What do you do?"

"I'm a filmmaker."

"I'm an actor," he grinned. "You wouldn't have a role for me in your next film, would you?"

I smiled at the incongruity of the situation. "You bet!" I replied, not missing a beat. Mostly so he wouldn't look through my suitcase packed with *saucisson*, pâté and cheese. He scribbled his email on the back of my customs declaration and handed it to me with a hearty, "Welcome home!"

• • •

Marc returns a month later. He helps Mohammad fill out an application for political asylum and takes him to nearby Metz to turn it in at City Hall. After four hours, Mohammad's number is called by a woman in her fifties with a stern expression. "You have a visa, that's already something."

"Yes, I was an interpreter with the French army."

"Hats off, you're a brave young man."

She hands him a voucher and explains he will soon be summoned by OFPRA (the French office for the protection of refugees and stateless persons) for an interview. In the meantime, the voucher will double as a residence permit. It's valid for 90 days and renewable until he receives a reply.

It's the start of a new ordeal. It takes months before he gets an appointment. The summons is sent to the wrong address, which means renewing the voucher more than once. Each time, he waits in line for hours to deal with racist civil servants getting their kicks out of humiliating him. Iran, Afghanistan, Sri Lanka and now France. Is he eternally condemned to be treated as less than human?

On April 4, 2015, he is summoned to City Hall. The letter stipulates it concerns his resident permit, but it doesn't specify whether his request has been granted or refused. He's heard horror stories of refugees who get arrested when they turned up for this sort of appointment. He asks Marc to come along, in case things go awry.

He takes a number and sits in the waiting room among dozens of men, women and children. How many will be allowed to stay? How many will get sent back to a country they fled, often at risk to their lives? Marc reassures him. With his application, he shouldn't have any trouble getting his papers. That's what the army in Kabul promised, it's what the UN personnel in Columbo said. Why should it be any different this time?

Number 058—Window 12. Mohammad walks up to the civil servant who invites him to sit down. He states his identity. The man disappears into an office then comes back with an envelope. He hands it to Mohammad.

"Your resident permit and travel document. With these, you can travel freely outside of France. The documents are valid for ten years."

For the first time since he left Kabul, Mohammad is sure he won't get sent back to his country. He won't have to hide anymore; he doesn't have to feel scared every time he encounters a policeman; he can even travel. It's a monumental relief.

But Mohammad is bored in Sarrebourg. Ever since Marc left on yet another mission to the Middle East, he's at loose ends. He has no friends and doesn't speak French. He wants to go to Paris. He wants to study, get back into music, give meaning to his life.

The only person he knows in Paris is Safi, a former interpreter for the French army. Safi warns him that life in the big city is hard. Expensive, too. "Are you sure it's the right choice?"

"Absolutely."

In late December, Mohammad takes a train to Paris. He's struck by all the colors, wealth, and abundance of Christmas decorations. The streets are packed with people, and the diversity is new to him. His heart pounds. This is the place for him.

Safi lives in a shelter in the 15th *arrondisement*. He offers to let Mohammad sleep at the foot of his bed on a blanket. He's been in France for eight months but still hasn't been granted refugee status. If his request is refused, he'll become an illegal alien liable to be deported; knowing a return to Kabul is nothing short of a death sentence. Is there no communication between the French government and its army? The military was the first to warn them of the danger they were in. But here, everyone appears to have forgotten how they served France. They're treated like outcasts. The only thing that seems to matter for the administration is not granting visas to refugees who lied about their condition. Shouldn't someone who left their country, family, friends, and everything else behind be considered a victim rather than a thief?

Mohammad spends his days wandering around Paris in search of a place to live. After a few weeks, he shifts his focus to the suburbs, since all the shelters within the city limits are swamped. He takes the commuter train out of town, every day to conduct his search, but keeps coming up empty-handed. Each night, he returns exhausted to Safi's tiny, overheated room. The two makeshift friends talk late into the night drinking lukewarm beer.

One morning, the director of the shelter throws Mohammad out for no clear reason, claiming a security issue. He threatens to kick Safi out, as well, if Mohammad doesn't leave immediately.

Mohammad finds himself out in the street. He sleeps here and there, wherever he can. In a park, under a bridge, on a street corner or in a metro station. More than once, he gets kicked out by subway security guards. Because he's clean and courteous, he never has any real trouble. After a while, he finds a nook at the entrance of a tunnel. It's noisy but hidden from view, and it offers protection in bad weather.

In the street, passersby stare at him or insult him for no reason. One day, while dozing on a bench, someone kicks him, and he falls right off. He wakes with a start to see two youths walking away, laughing.

Little by little, Mohammad is drained of strength and courage. He dreams of having somewhere he can settle down and finally start thinking about the future.

We toss our cigar butts into the flowerbed beside the house and put the lawn chairs back into the shed.

We've never spent so much time together. Before this project, I'd only bump into Mohammad when I would come to Paris. It was always brief. We'd exchange a few words, nothing very personal. I'd never taken the time to learn more about him, attributing his presence to my mother's new whim. Since she hadn't bothered consulting me when she made the decision to take him in, I didn't feel very concerned. Besides, Mohammad would probably be gone the next time I visited, so why grow attached?

I make the rounds of the house, scatter the coals in the fireplace, put the protective screen in front of the hearth, gather the bottles and glasses, and turn out the light in the living room.

Then I tackle the dishes. Mohammad joins me in the kitchen. He pours himself another glass of wine, leans against the windowsill and continues his story.

Methodically, he visits every shelter in the Parisian area. One morning, he takes the train out to Melun. He's heard of a shelter for mentally disabled teens and former drug addicts that might have a bed available. He's a little frightened by the prospect but is desperate to find somewhere to live before winter. An hour later, he arrives.

The director grills him about his past, eyes him from head to toe, then announces he has a spot for him. He hands Mohammad a list of the house rules:

—Residents must be in by 7:00 pm
—Residents may not go out on weekends without
 special permission.
—For all activities outside the shelter, a letter of
 request must be presented to the director who has
 the right to accept or refuse without explanation.
—Residents must provide advance warning if they

want to eat at the shelter (if they change their mind,
they won't have a meal).
—Wake-up at 6:30 am
—Curfew at 9:00 pm
—Showers every other day.
—Any violation of the rules results in expulsion.

A social worker leads him to a cold, impersonal room with bunkbeds. His roommate Alex, 24, is tall, skinny, uncommunicative and bipolar.

Mohammad finds himself lumped in with the delinquants and disabled teens at the shelter. He gets treated like a child, like someone who is ill. The cafeteria meals are prepared with expired goods from local supermarkets. He often finds flies or worms in his food. But he doesn't dare complain, afraid of getting kicked out.

The staff are manipulative and cruel, frequently mistreating the people they are supposedly caring for. Worst of all is the director. A real sadist. He takes a dislike to Mohammad from the very first day and never lets up, constantly giving orders in French, knowing Mohammad can't understand. Mohammad forces himself to remain polite and, even the most outlandish requests, merely replies, "With pleasure."

"Who said anything about pleasure? Just do what I say!"

Despite Mohammad's efforts, the director unfailingly refuses to let him leave the shelter on weekends, forcing him instead to clean the common areas while other residents visit their families.

One Saturday night, when the two are alone, the director asks Mohammad about his plans for the future. After a moment's hesitation, Mohammad decides to speak openly. He talks about his love for rap and music in general, and how he hopes to get involved in it again soon. "I'd also like to go to school. As soon as my French is better, I plan to apply to college."

The director bursts out laughing. "You're completely nuts! Do you think that's how it works here? This is France, not some backass country. Look at me, I've worked in this dump for 30 years, and it's taken me this long to get my car, my house and my vacation by the sea.

You think you can just waltz in, snap your fingers and get all that? You haven't a clue, boy." And with that, he disappears into his office.

Mohammad is stunned. Tears stream down his cheeks. He is torn between shame and rage. He has half a mind to kick the door down and jam a pen into the guy's neck. But he takes a deep breath and calms himself down. He knows that in the blink of an eye, he could wind up out on the street again. And the slightest brush with the law would land him on a one-way flight back to Kabul.

The residents seem nice enough, but Mohammad avoids spending time with them. They have no goals, no drive, no dreams, and he can feel their influence rubbing off on him. His mental state is fragile, and he knows it's bad for him to have too much contact with them.

Besides providing a roof over their heads, the shelter is supposed to offer training courses. Mohammad wants to study French. Not speaking the language is a major handicap, but all the classes are full. The only course available is called *Maximizing your resume*. Mohammad finds himself alone in a room with a computer, a sheet of paper and a pencil. He has no idea what he is supposed to do. He figures an instructor will appear. He waits half-an-hour but no one shows up. He steps out of the room, but the director is in the hallway and merely orders him back inside. Mohammad complies, sits down at the computer and starts surfing the web. He finds several language courses in the Paris area, but he's stuck in the suburbs. Except for lunch in the cafeteria, he isn't allowed out of this room until 5:00 pm By then, it's too late to take the train into Paris. Mohammad knows if he misses curfew, he'll be kicked out.

How can he find a job without speaking French? How can he learn French without leaving the shelter? How can he get out of the shelter without a place to live? How can he get a place to live without making money? How can he make money without a job?

He has to get out. He makes more and more calls to associations specialized in helping refugees. The people he speaks to are attentive and understanding, but no one has a concrete solution The best they can do is offer him theater or pottery classes.

He asks to speak to the director and is given an appointment a few days later.

"If you can't help me, at least let me find a solution on my own. I need to be able to come and go from the shelter. I have to go to Paris in order to take French classes. Won't you give me permission to be late from time to time?"

"There are rules. If I start making exceptions for you, why not for everyone else?"

"That's absurd. Not everyone has the same needs."

"If you don't like it, you can leave. Find a job and rent a room. For the time being, as long as you're here, I make the rules."

"Can't you see I'm not like the other residents? I'm not an addict, I'm not mentally disabled, and I haven't broken any laws. I'm a refugee. I left my country because I had no choice, it was a matter of life or death. I had everything I needed there to be happy. A good job, family, friends. So, stop talking to me like I'm worthless. It's insulting to be treated like that."

The director storms out and slams the door behind him.

Mohammad has just turned 20 and is losing hope. He's been living in the shelter for three months, and every day the future looks bleaker and bleaker.

All this time, he's never given up, always believing he'd be able to go to school one day, perhaps even start a family. But for the first time, he wonders if those aren't just pipe dreams. Maybe none of it will ever happen. Perhaps he'll be condemned to spend the rest of his life moving from shelter to shelter, at the mercy of mediocre, racist, selfish people. Relying on the charity of a few kind souls. Wandering aimlessly with no hope or joy. Surviving.

● ● ●

I finish rinsing the glasses, turn out the lights, lock the door and hide the key. We climb into the car and hit the road for Paris.

As I drive, I think back over the day we've just spent together. When we entered the house that morning, I knew nothing about Mohammad. A few hours, beers, cocktails and cigars later, I know more than most people he's encountered in his life. It strikes me this is the first time someone's opened to me like this. Such an avalanche of information all at once makes my head spin. We spend most of our lives among by people we know almost everything about. It's reassuring. But it can also get boring. I remember a few years ago, I started to feel a bit world-weary. I was surrounded by people I deeply loved, happy to be able to see them regularly, but it was getting repetitive. The same discussions, the same faces. This is one of the reasons I decided to move across the Atlantic. I liked the idea of making new friends, discovering new lives and stories. When we arrived in Brooklyn, we took things slowly. The kids needed us to help make the great leap; and after 20 years together, Eleonore and I were glad to have some time for just the two of us. Little by little, we started meeting people and learned a multitude of unusual stories. It's been one of the most exciting things about living abroad. Today, when I go back to Paris, it's an immense joy to spend time with my family and friends. We see each other less, but it's more intense when we do.

We speed along the highway in the dark. "What would you have done if you were me?" Mohammad asks.

"In your position?"

"If you were an Afghan refugee?"

"I can't answer that question. I'm a 47-year-old man, born in France to a well-to-do family. I've never gone hungry or had to fight to survive, or for my freedom. I've never been on my own. It's pointless for me to pretend to be in your shoes. My instinct, all my reflexes and reasoning are rooted in a life that's too different from yours."

We fall silent. The sound of the engine fills the car.

One night, like every other night, my mother is listening to the radio and leafing through a magazine. Its cover promises in bold typeface to reveal: *The 100 Secrets of the Most Stylish Women Around the World*. Claire Rodier, an immigration lawyer, is on the air.

"Western populations are increasingly isolationist. We're at war with men and women who are dying of hunger. As if it were a crime to seek a better life or merely try to survive, in a country other than one's own."

She points out the total number of refugees, in the 28-member nations of the European Union, is equal to the number that Pakistan alone welcomes in. Recently, the president of the European Commission decided to make member nations face up to their responsibilities. Each must accept a certain quota of the 2 million refugees in Turkey, knowing more and more arrive each day. EU countries started bargaining pathetically to take in as few as possible, citing excuses such as economic woes, too many refugees already, local resistance, etc. After two months of negotiations, they finally agreed on the measly number of 60,000 refugees for all of Europe.

My mother looks out the window, taking in some air.

Now a young man is talking. He works for Singa, an association that helps migrants.

"Our organization was founded in 2012 and sprang from the experience of two people: Nathanael, a legal assistant for asylum seekers and refugees in Morocco; and me, Guillaume, in Australia. As lawyers, we both experienced the same thing, but 10,000 miles apart. Migrants would come into our office and say, 'I want to continue my career as a cabinetmaker: I want to start my own business,' or 'I want to make friends.' The only thing we could offer was a report on the human-rights situation in their country. We felt completely useless, like we had zero impact on their lives. We were meeting people with extraordinary backgrounds, who weren't able to do anything, concretely speaking. For example, there was a Syrian who'd been a nose in a perfumery in Aleppo, a man with exceptional talent; but since he had no contacts in his field, he wound up having to revert to construction work. We saw this kind of thing daily, and we felt people ought to be aware of it. People had to stop looking at migrants as freeloaders. We realized what these men and women really needed was a way to meet people and make connections. So, we started organizing events to put them in contact with people on all different horizons; they could go dancing together, play soccer or have a picnic. Without someone being there to give and others to receive. No beneficiaries, no volunteers. It wasn't about showing solidarity with the refugees, but sharing a good time, which went both ways. Not vertically, when someone is above or below; rather, horizontally, meaning on the same level. We looked for participants everywhere we could: in shelters, in the street, among our friends. It was magical. For the first time, they felt like themselves. Like they weren't wearing a label. People opened, they talked to us about their aspirations: one wanted to start a foodtruck; another dreamed of working in fashion; another had an engineering degree. Then we came up with the idea of putting immigrants in contact with people who had the capacity of housing someone. In no time, we were swamped. In just a few months, we got 10,000 offers for accommodations throughout France. From Dunkerque to Bastia, from Brest to Strasbourg, from every social sphere—policemen, students, entrepreneurs. People were prepared to share houseboats, manors, attics, whatever they could offer."

"Do you feel that if you can help, you must help?" the interviewer asked. "Lots of people could, yet don't do anything."

"We try as hard as we can not to make people feel guilty. But it's true that if everyone who had the means got involved, the disastrous situation we're in today would completely change."

If you can, you must. It's a jolt for my mother. She can't go on doing nothing. She's fortunate enough to have a large home with the capacity to host someone inside.

She reaches for a scrap of paper on the nightstand and jots down the name of the association: Singa.

The next morning, she goes online to find out more. Singa's website looks nice, is easy to navigate and seems credible. She clicks on *I would like to host someone in my home.* A questionnaire pops up.

She fills it out. Gender, first and last name, date and place of birth, address and phone. Then:

—*Marital status* > Married in 1968—Widowed in 2010
—*Children* > three sons (47, 45 and 42 years old)
                 seven grandchildren
—*Languages spoken* > French, English, Spanish
—*Field* > Fashion
—*Professional situation* > Created two businesses
  with my husband which we sold. New projects
  in the works.
—*Would you be willing to share your professional*
  skills with the person you host? > Yes
—*Would you be willing to use your connections to*
  help the person you host professionally? > Yes
—*Interests* > Art, cinema, literature, cooking
—*Tell us about yourself* > I like life, people, doing and
  sharing. I'm avid, artistic, scatterbrained but
  responsible. I love to love, I'm fascinated by beauty,
  hate conflict, can't imagine heart without smarts,
  solemnity without humor, and *joie de vivre* without
  courage. I'm creative and continue to work. I go out
  frequently, travel, and have a large family.
—*What are your motivations for hosting someone and*
  what do you expect to get out of the experience? >
  How can someone be so fortunate and happy, yet
  tolerate so much misery? Thank you, Singa, for
  giving us the opportunity to be a little less selfish and
  providing the joy of seeing lives begin again.
—*When can you begin hosting?* > Immediately
—*For how long?* > One year (to start with)
—*How many people can you host?* > One (to start with)

She clicks on "register" and immediately receives an email confirmation. She calls the number on the document to find out how long it will take. The person on the phone greets her with a, "Wow, you're so cool!" Young people, clearly, which she finds both refreshing and a bit worrisome. What is she getting into? She's torn between feeling good about doing something, and doubts about getting in over her head. She wonders if she's completely nuts. Does she really want a stranger in her house?

Days and weeks go by. After two months, still no news. She's surprised to feel secretly relieved.

On the TV, men, women, and children are walking through a German train station, as a small group welcomes them with applause. The caption: *Munich inhabitants greet migrants. Germany predicts 10,000 to arrive this Sunday.* On screen, a refugee says, "I feel good. Like I can finally breathe." Mohammad sits on his own watching the old television bolted to one of the grey walls in the shelter's common area. He is mesmerized. He thinks about how the images of adversity and suffering, constantly broadcast by the media, accentuate the impression of sub-humanity. It's humiliating for people who view themselves as exceptional for having survived such terrible things. It discredits the courage and strength it took to face so many obstacles. German Chancellor Angela Merkel comes on to announce she's opening her country's borders to hundreds of thousands of refugees. "I'll do everything in my power to give protection to those who need protection. We must give a friendly welcome to people who, for the most part, are in critical situations. Fences serve no purpose. They're pointless. It's important that every person be treated like a human being."

Unfortunately, outcry over the decision in the rest of Europe and other EU countries' refusal to follow her lead eventually force Merkel to take back those statements.

With all Mohammad's searching on the Internet, he finally comes across the Singa website. He discovers a program called Calm (*Comme à la Maison*—meaning *like at home*) that offers to find lodging for refugees "in someone's home." He contacts the association and tells them he'll go anywhere to get out of the squalid shelter. The place is making him sick. For the past few days, he's had a terrible headache. A migraine that just keeps getting worse. As if someone were sticking a screwdriver into the back of his skull.

He decides to skip his training and go to Paris to meet the people running the association. He hops on the commuter train then changes to the subway. When he comes out onto the street, he crosses a man who smiles at him. It's been ages since a stranger has shown him any kindness. Is it a sign? When he reaches the Singa offices, he's greeted by Sarah, a volunteer not much older than himself. She asks about his centers of interest, his hopes and dreams. It's been forever since anyone's asked Mohammad these things, and he struggles to reply intelligibly. He's afraid she'll interpret his incoherence as lack of motivation. To make up for it, he relates the odyssey that took him from Kabul to Paris via Colombo. "See? I am motivated!"

Sarah reassures him she's not there to judge. She's only trying to learn as much as she can about him to be able to "pair" him with the right person. She's hopeful. It's much easier for a man alone—a young man who speaks a little French—to find a place to live than a whole family who's just arrived. She promises to call him as soon as she has something to offer.

Back at the shelter, the director threatens to kick him out. Mohammad keeps a low profile and continues to spend his days alone at the computer, putting up with the sarcasm and humiliation while awaiting the call that would save his life.

• • •

I want to know more.

On one of my visits to Paris, I make an appointment to see one of the two founders of Singa.

The association is located at the back of a courtyard in a dozen offices with glass walls. It's filled with men and women of all ages, volunteers and migrants who've come looking for information or just a bit of comfort. A man in his thirties, Guillaume, receives me in the main room, a common area where people can meet for coffee, enjoy a cookie or read the paper.

He introduces me to Hamze, a Persian-looking man slightly older than himself, who greets me, fetches a glass of water and goes back to his computer. Guillaume says Hamze is from Iran and has been part of Singa since it began. From the very start, they decided to chart the highs and lows in the life of everyone they work with, to get a better grasp of their journeys. A striking drop appears in the middle of Hamze's story. He was a politician back in Tehran, having slowly climbed the ladder to become an adviser to the Prime Minister. Then came the elections and a change of regime, and Hamze found himself thrown in prison. At that point, his career ground to a halt. When he got out of prison, he figured it was time to leave the country. He flew to France. And that's when the curve took a nosedive once he reached Paris. How could French hospitality be worse than an Iranian prison? "Back there, I had my dignity. I expressed my ideas and was imprisoned for it. At least in a conflict, you have human relationships with the people you're fighting. In France, I was nothing anymore. A nobody. I faced utter indifference. There's nothing worse than that."

Guillaume opens his laptop and pulls up their homepage. Their activity has three focuses. The first: to provide information, both for refugees—explaining French social codes (why people kiss cheeks, why they shake hands, etc.) —as well as for French citizens, constantly bombarded with truncated, limited and negative news portraying migrants as a homogenous mass flooding into their country to take advantage of the system. To fight these prejudices, Singa spreads the message that the people lined up outside City Hall aren't merely asking for something. They also have a past, present, and future. They each have their own story. Unlike most media, which talks about potential terrorism, poverty, and instability, we try to imagine a bright future for these individuals. The association insists that a refugee is not just a refugee; but a carpenter, a cook, a scientist, a farmer, an athlete, and so on.

Guillaume clicks on another page and pictures of people from all over the world appear.

Their second focus is putting new arrivals in contact with locals who share the same passions. Soccer fans, if possible, supporters of the same team, movie buffs, rock climbing enthusiasts, engineers who can give each other precious contacts.

"These partnerships have led to businesses, music bands, and even relationships. I met a 20-year-old man from Pakistan who'd never spoken to a woman outside his own family. In a French association, 90% of the employees are female. He couldn't get any information because he thought he wasn't allowed to talk to the women. Our role is to identify this sort of difficulty and make the connection easier."

He closes his laptop and turns to me. "As time goes by, we find ourselves increasingly in an administrative and legal system focused on relief and security. The model needs to be reevaluated. We have to change the conversation from, "Refugees are a homogenous group that do this or that..." to "I met Ahmed; he has an idea and I'm going to try to help him." Instead of saying we're going to take in the world's misery, which is discouraging and counter-productive, we present individuals and activities on a human scale. We have several new projects. For instance, we're developing a video game. Thirty five million French people play video games. Instead of giving conferences on political asylum, which draw a hundred stragglers at best, our aim is to reach as many people as we can. And in order to optimize our Calm program that puts refugees in contact with people who can host them, we're developing a website that operates like online dating. Because the problem today is that we're currently only present in four cities in France, whereas refugees and potential hosts are spread throughout the country."

This young man fascinates me. For years I've felt discouraged about the lack of political engagement among younger generations. The rates of abstentionism grow higher with every election, especially among this population bracket. They no longer believe in the Messiah, political parties or the old patterns. And a lot of them are getting involved out in the field, to make up for their disillusionment. They wager on changing society through concrete action, rather than through elaborate displays of decrees and laws.

What Guillaume and his associates have done is garnering attention from political authorities. The Ministry of Housing has just put out a call for proposals based on the same blueprint as Calm. The MEDEF (Movement of the Enterprises of France) is showing an interest in the entrepreneurial spirit of migrants, creating programs specifically geared toward them. Paris' City Hall has also gotten on board. And during the last presidential election campaign, Benoît Hamon, the Socialist Party candidate, visited the Singa offices. He walked in saying how important it was "to help," how he wanted "to help," and that he thought he was "helping." They told him that when we want to do something "for," we often sidestep the people concerned, with their specific qualities, and that it's better to do something "with." After this, Hamon modified his program.

The people at the helm of the association have realized that, despite malfunctions in the way migrants are welcomed today in France, there's no point denouncing them; it's better to try to create inspiring models so everyone can seize those tools and take action themselves, in ministries, neighborhoods, and businesses. It's a long-term strategy that's beginning to bear fruit. For example, they've just been contacted by Airbnb, asking about ways to help refugees after Trump took office.

"If a company of that size starts getting involved, we're no longer talking about hundreds of places to live, but millions. And that's a total game changer. If we allow ourselves to be optimistic, we could even imagine it will change the world balance."

His enthusiasm is contagious. What if the grassroots took over and managed to counterbalance governments' disastrous immigration policies? If *we the people* could make up for public authorities' lack of involvement throughout the world by each getting involved on our own level—from the shepherd in the Alps who helps a migrant family cross an obsolete border pass, to the vacation rental giant ready to put empty homes at the disposal of the homeless, no matter what their origins?

"I believe in the future. It's long, painstaking work. We plant seeds, and though you can't see anything yet, the day it bears fruit, it's going to be huge. The problem is the media constantly undermines our work. We're continuously swimming upstream, and it's exhausting. Articles always state *Juliette and Gerard took in a refugee*, but never *Juliette and Gerard took in Ahmed*, and even less, *Ahmed was taken in by a French couple*. Another edifying example: Amnesty International ran a study to find out how many French people would be willing to host a refugee in their homes. Nine percent replied yes. The press ran a huge headline: *Less than 10% of French people are ready to host a refugee in their home!* Whereas we're talking about six million French people— that's amazing! The papers should have written, *Six million French people are ready to host a refugee in their home!*"

My mother is in her garden, absorbed in a novel from her personal collection—piles of books stacked up on either side of her bed. She's curious and always buys a lot more than she can ever read. My mother is a bookshop's dream, a publisher's fantasy, and every writer's favorite target.

That day, the winner is Erri de Luca, her favorite Italian author. *Il Più e il Meno* [The Most and the Least] peeked out of the pile at her.

On Sunday, we would have lunch at Nonna Emma's, my mother's mother. Since Friday night, she'd been taking turns with her daughter-in-law Lillina before the tiny flame where the stew was simmering.

The sauce was a standing ovation after a goal, an embrace, an olfactory leap and somersault.

There, at Emma and Lillina's home, I was given detailed information about the composition of eggplant parmesan, my favorite meal as an adult. To prepare it, the vegetable was submitted to three heat sources. They would slice the eggplants and set them in the sun, the most powerful heat of all, to dry out the water and intensify the taste. Then they would fry them, gilding the kitchen with a festive color. The final heat was the oven, after layering the slices, smothering each with tomato sauce, basil, mozzarella and a handful of parmesan. Three heats contributed to the dish that came the closest in my mind to the word "home."

My mother smiles. Cooking and literature, the pinnacles of her happiness. Her phone rings.

"Hello, this is Catherine Halard. I'm a volunteer with Singa. I'm looking at your file here. Are you still willing to host someone at your home?"

"Um... Yes, of course."

"Great. When would you be able to meet Mohammad?"

My mother suggests the next day at the brasserie near her home. She hangs up and rests the book on her lap. Is she prepared to open her home to a stranger she's only talked to for ten minutes in a café? She needs to know him better than that before handing over her keys. She decides to suggest a deal. She will pay for a hotel room in the neighborhood for a week, and they can spend time together during the day. Once they've gotten to know each other, he can move in.

What would my father say if he were still around? The man was so attached to his peace and quiet, he certainly would have discouraged her. And what if it doesn't work out? Would she dare send the young man back out onto the street? Does she really want the bother of a stranger's presence everyday? It could soon become constraining, annoying even. It isn't too late to change her mind. She glances at the large dwelling encircling the garden. *When you can, you must.* She takes a long sip of cold water and goes back to her book, trying to focus on the recipe for eggplant *alla parmigiana*.

• • •

Mohammad is bored to tears. For an hour, he's been sitting alone in a large room waiting for an instructor who's supposed to teach him accounting basics. Despite his claims he has better things to do than learn *the art of recording, classifying and summarizing in a significant manner and in terms of money, transactions and events which are of financial character, and interpreting the results thereof*, they wouldn't listen. He isn't allowed to leave the room and has to suffer in silence. He doesn't even have the energy to go online to look for other shelters or associations that might help him. Now that he's gone through the whole list of the ones in the Paris region, he could try his luck in another town; but the thought of leaving the big city completely depresses him. Lost in thought, he doesn't hear his phone vibrating in his backpack. The caller insists and this time Mohammad answers.

"This is Catherine," a husky voice announces. "I work for the association Singa. You enrolled in our program?"

"Yes."

"Are you still looking for a place to live?"

"Yes."

"I have good news: someone's willing to take you."

"What do you mean take me?"

"Host you in their home."

"Really?"

"Yes, but we need to act fast. Are you in Paris?"

"No, Melun."

"Can you come to Paris tomorrow morning?"

"No, I'm only allowed out on weekends."

"Ah. That's a problem. The lady in question usually spends weekends in the country. Maybe you could put someone in charge on the line so I can explain the situation?"

"No, I'd rather not."

"We need to jump on this. There are lots of candidates."

"Alright, don't worry. I'll sort it out. Tell me when and where. I'll be there."

He hangs up and whoops with joy. The director bursts into the room. "What's going on?"

Mohammad smiles.

"You scared me, you idiot," he glares.

Mohammad ventures, "Can I skip class tomorrow morning, just for once?"

"Out of the question."

"I have an appointment with someone who might have a place for me to live in Paris."

"If you miss a session, don't bother coming back."

The next morning, Mohammad picks out his nicest clothes, gulps down a cup of coffee in the cafeteria and heads to accounting class like every day. After about 30 minutes, he asks the instructor for permission to go to the restroom. He leaves the room, walks nonchalantly to the exit and out the door. Once he is through the gate, he hastens to the train station.

His room will be gone when he comes back, but he knows this is his last chance.

My mother listens to her favorite radio station as she enjoys breakfast in bed: a cup of tea and half a grapefruit. It's almost summer and she's being careful. My mother's been on a diet for 40 years and knows it will never end. She's too much of a foodie to resist the good things in life, so this is her price to pay not to completely lose control.

She carefully picks out her clothes. It's an important meeting. What happens today is going to change the life of the young man she hasn't met yet, and will no doubt shake up her own, as well.

Mohammad sits in the middle of the car. His headache came back the minute he boarded the commuter train. The pain is unbearable. He presses his face against the window to cool it down. He prays Marie-France will speak English, and that he'll be able to express himself clearly—despite his head feeling like it's in a vice grip. He hopes he'll make a good impression in his unironed clothes. That he'll manage to hide his sadness and despair. He keeps repeating to himself, "Be honest, be yourself."

Catherine, an elegant woman in her sixties, offered to meet my mother an hour before Mohammad's arrival, to explain things. She's been volunteering with Singa for six months and has already found lodging for 15 migrants. Most of the time it goes well, even if there've been a few unfortunate experiences. Like for instance, the elderly lady who agreed to host a young man who then showed up with two friends. She said no but they insisted, claiming her spare bedroom was certainly big enough for three. They grew aggressive, she got frightened and withdrew her offer to host.

"Why are you telling me this?"

"I want to be honest with you. Sometimes there are incompatibilities, but we're here to resolve any potential conflicts. For example, there's a case of a famous writer who wanted to host a Syrian and got upset when we paired him with a Rwandan. The Syrian refugee crisis was at its height, and he probably thought it was more meritable to host a teenager from Aleppo, than a young woman from a country no one cared about anymore. She was 31 and spoke fluent French but was prone to depression. She'd spend all day in her room watching TV shows on her computer. The office where he wrote was right next to her bedroom, and it got on his nerves. Things quickly grew tense between them and it ended badly. What he said to her was awful: 'What bothers me most is to think my taxes pay for your welfare, and here I am, a socialist.' In the end, another family took her in, and it went really well. It's not individual personalities that matter, it's compatibility."

They order another coffee. My mother is curious. Is there a certain profile for the typical host? No, it varies. And how does she pair people up? She makes two columns on an Excel document: the names of refugees on the right, the host candidates on the left, all sorted by age, and in the middle, everyone's interests. Then she connects those who have the most in common.

Catherine was particularly moved by Mohammad's profile; he is the exact same age as her youngest son. She thought his interest in fashion and intellectual curiousity would fit nicely with my mother's love for literature and film. She usually tries to put people of the same age together and avoids putting a woman alone with a single man; but in this case, she felt he needed a maternal figure.

"Where is he living right now?"

"In a shelter outside Paris for young drug addicts and mentally disabled teens."

My mother is troubled by this. She tells Catherine how she plans to put Mohammad up in a hotel for a week to get to know him better before letting him stay in her home. Catherine thinks it's a good idea.

The two of them really hit it off. My mother asks Catherine if she's ever hosted a migrant herself.

"I'm very involved in the association, but I'm ashamed to say, I'm too selfish to host someone in my own home. My youngest son has just moved out, and my husband and I are finally on our own. We're simply not ready to have a third person under our roof again. It's true, I feel like I'm doing things halfway. I feel guilty, but everyone does what they can. I give my time; others give money or a place to stay. A lot of people do it to feel better about themselves, but that doesn't matter. I often attend group meetings where host families talk about their experiences. Most people admit it gives them a sense of self-worth and makes them look good in the eyes of others. So much the better."

Mohammad enters the café. Catherine waves to him. He walks slowly up to the two women smiling at him, trying his best to mask exhaustion and fear. He doesn't want to go back to the shelter; he doesn't want to sleep on the streets anymore; he yearns for gentleness and love.

He greets them politely then excuses himself to wash his hands.

My mother was expecting someone with dark skin and a dark beard. Instead, she finds herself before a 20-year-old man with the face of an angel, light skin, almond eyes, and jet black hair. She immediately remarks on his red down jacket and matching new Converse sneakers. She's very attentive to people's footwear. She would rather see someone dressed poorly with nice shoes than the other way around.

Catherine interrupts her thoughts. "Oh yes, I forgot. The association advises hosts not to ask the refugees too much about their past the first time they meet. We don't want to destabilize them."

Mohammad returns, shakes hands and sits down across from them.

"Hello, Mohammad, I'm Marie-France." My mother's voice is gentle, her English very proper.

"Nice to meet you."

"So, tell me, how did you get here?"

Catherine shoots her a dark look. My mother smiles. She needs to know. She's about to welcome a stranger into her home and doesn't give a fig about the association's rules. Soon it will be just Mohammad and her.

They talk for ten minutes or so. Mohammad gives a brief summary of his trajectory in a neutral voice. His collaboration with the French army, then his troubles since he arrived in France. My mother asks what he wants to do now. He says the most important things for him are going to school and continuing to make music. Of course, he'll have to work for a living, but he hopes to be able to go to college.

"I'd like to study political science. My dream is to go to Science Po."

My mother smiles. It's nice to dream.

She compliments him on his outfit. He admits it's his secret passion. He's always loved nice fabrics and good cuts.

"What do you need most today?"

"A place where I can settle, sleep, and find peace."

"I'm ready to host you, but there's no freedom without money. I'll give you a room and also find you a job. I'm counting on you not to let me down."

Mohammad's eyes sparkle. He peers at my mother in silence. He slowly repeats those six magic words in his head: I. Am. Ready. To. Host. You. He tries to keep his composure, but what he really wants is to hug Marie-France, kiss Catherine, dance with the waiter, yelp with joy, and run naked down the street.

"When would you like to come?"

"As soon as possible."

"Go get your things. I'll be waiting for you at home."

On the train back to Melun, Mohammad slowly catches his breath. He reaches into his pocket and pulls out the scrap of paper that Marie-France scribbled her address on. It suddenly hits him that she lives between the Invalides and the Eiffel Tower, a couple minutes from the Musée de l'Armée. He can hardly believe it. He had no idea where they had met was right next door to her home where he would soon be living.

He reaches the shelter. All he wants is to grab his stuff and get out of there without a fuss. As soon as he walks into the building, one of the social workers makes a beeline for him. The guy's furious. He asks Mohammad where he's been all morning. Mohammad simply states he's leaving. Impossible. He must wait for the director. Mohammad ignores him and goes to gather his things. When he comes back to the reception desk, the director still isn't there. He needs to sign Mohammad's authorization to leave. Two monitors stand at the front door blocking the exit. An hour goes by. It's getting dark. Marie-France must wonder what he's doing. Maybe she's gone out to dinner or to meet someone. Will she still be home when he arrives? He pulls out the slip of paper with her address, to see if there's a phone number on it. No such luck. When the monitors are distracted a moment, Mohammad sneaks out of the building and dashes to the train station. He buys a ticket and walks all the way to the end of the platform, as far from the station entrance as possible. He keeps glancing back anxiously toward the stairs. No one. He's still naive enough to believe they really care. Would they actually bother chasing after him? He doesn't even exist to them; or to anyone, for that matter. The train appears.

I'm in Brooklyn. It's Indian summer, my favorite time of year. I have lunch with my daughter, Philomene, on the terrace of the little Mediterranean restaurant on the corner of our block. She's just started college and is complaining about the lack of privacy in the dorm room she shares with two other students. The girls are nice, but it's hard to focus on her work, and there's no privacy when her boyfriend Charlie comes to visit. They'd like to rent a studio together in Bushwick. When we visited the campus, it almost made me want to go back to school to experience dorm life for myself, a world away from parents and daily problems. But clearly, it's not all it's cracked up to be. She wants her own place. She's 18, after all. If she found a little part-time job, she could help out with rent. It's a deal. I go home and before getting back to work, I phone my mother for our weekly chat. It's 8:30 pm in Paris, the perfect time for a family debriefing. Basically, all news about my brothers and the rest of the clan comes through her. From time to time, I ask for her advice or share my concerns.

"Ah, hello Benoit, honey."

"How are you?" I hear the radio in the background. "What are you up to tonight?"

"I'm waiting for Mohammad. I'm worried, he should have been here already."

"Who?"

Mohammad pushes open the heavy door of the building. He walks through the lobby and reaches the gate of a small garden. He rings the intercom. My mother buzzes him in.

"I was worried."

"I'm sorry. They didn't want to let me out back at the shelter."

"What did you do?"

"I made a run for it."

She smiles knowingly, then notices his suitcase.

"Is that it for your belongings?"

"Yes."

"I really like your suitcase. It's lovely. Where did you get it?"

"In Colombo. Sri Lanka."

She shows him around the house. They walk through the entrance then the living room and into the kitchen. Mohammad takes in the high ceilings, vast rooms, beautiful furniture, large windows that look out onto the garden, and, above all, the feeling of warmth and comfort. It reminds him of the vast bourgeois houses of rich Iranian families, in posh neighborhoods of Isfahan he'd walk past on his way to school. Sometimes he'd catch a glimpse, through a bay window or a door left ajar, but figured he'd never set foot inside.

He's both excited and completely exhausted. He can tell my mother's surprised by his lack of enthusiasm, but he can't fool her. "It's too much. I didn't expect all this."

He promises himself he'll make up for it later, as soon as he feels better and has rested.

They go upstairs and enter a spacious room on the top floor of the house. A double bed, a wardrobe, a desk, and a few steps leading up to a private bathroom.

"This is your room."

Mohammad freezes.

"Do you like it?"

He blinks back tears. My mother comes over and gathers him in her arms. "Don't worry, everything's going to be fine."

Mohammad's lost. In shock. He can't wrap his mind around it. Yesterday he was in a dreary shelter out in the suburbs; today, a *hôtel particulier,* a beautiful mansion, in the 7th of Paris. For years he's muddled through, not knowing what tomorrow will bring. Each day was a new challenge and ordeal. It's been an eternity since he's had a place to call home. A century since he's had a rest. He can't believe this day has finally come. He's not prepared mentally and is in distress.

My mother suggests they go out for dinner. Mohammad turns her down. He's terribly sorry, but he's just too tired.

"We have all the time in the world. Get some rest."

Before she leaves the room, she gives him the code to the garden gate and tells him she never locks the house. My mother has spent her whole life trusting people, and, so far, it's turned out pretty well. She relies on her instinct and has faith her luck will hold. She refuses to let her life be dictated by fear.

• • •

Without unpacking, Mohammad lies down and stares a long while at the stars out the window of his new room. He's floating. Then suddenly, his aching head brings him back to reality. He thinks about his hasty departure from the shelter and decides to email the director. He gets off the bed and takes his laptop out of his bag. He apologizes for leaving in such a rush and gives his new address for forwarding his mail. Mohammad gloats at the thought of that scumbag's face, when he learns he now lives next to the Eiffel Tower. He gets a reply almost immediately. It's scathing. The director is absolutely furious. He upbraids him for not respecting the rules, and says he's alerted the authorities. He's made a list of all Mohammad's offenses over the past three months, and says he'll never be accepted again in any establishment in or around Paris. Mohammad is livid. He tosses and turns in bed, unable to fall asleep. Suddenly, he gets up, pulls on his clothes, and leaves the room. He creeps quietly down the stairs, slips outside, crosses the deserted street, and heads down into the subway. He has to change lines twice before he can get the commuter train out to Melun. When he gets off at the last stop, he's the only one on the platform. He leaves the station and walks through the dark to the shelter. He reaches the gate and rings the bell. No reply. Mohammad rings and rings and rings. After a few minutes, he hears swearing on the other side and footsteps approaching. The gate opens. The director stands there, hatred flashing in his eyes. Before he can even say a word, Mohammad punches him in the gut. The guy doubles over and crumples to his knees. Mohammad grabs him by the collar, drags him inside the courtyard, and pulls out a box cutter. The director whimpers and writhes. Mohammad slowly presses the blade to his neck. They both freeze.

"What are you going to do now?"

"I'm sorry. I'll withdraw the complaint; I'll tell them it was a mistake. I'll even write you a letter of recommendation if you want. I can..."

Mohammad is completely disgusted by this guy. With a quick jerk of the blade, he slits his throat. Blood gushes out like a geyser and showers Mohammad's face.

· · ·

My mother's prepared a gargantuan breakfast: hot chocolate, toast, croissants, scrambled eggs, bacon, and her famous raspberry jam. Mohammad doesn't know where to start.

"Do you eat bacon?"

"Sure, no problem. The only thing I don't eat is human flesh."

"How'd you sleep?"

"The bed's really comfortable, but I had a terrible nightmare."

He tells her about his nighttime jaunt out to the shelter, and how he slit the director's throat. Then he digs into the pastries. A weighty silence fills the kitchen. My mother stares at her half-grapefruit, methodically detaching the sections with a little serrated silver spoon, designed just for that purpose.

"I'm going to make a few phone calls so you can start working as soon as possible."

"Thank you." He polishes off his eggs and goes back to his room.

My mother calls Richard, her psychiatrist friend. "I suppose it's normal for him to have nightmares, but this one was really violent."

"Dreams are characteristic of PTSD. Survivors relive an attack or extremely harrowing situation they've been through. It's the very definition of a nightmare. The dreams can recur every night, and some people start to avoid sleep for fear of reliving the scenes. They put off going to bed as long as they can. The vivid nightmares of PTSD are often more harrowing than reality. They're like hallucinations, in that they seem more intense than reality. In life, there's always the shadow of a doubt. But in a hallucination, there's not the slightest uncertainty. People suffering from post-traumatic stress relive the horrific scenes they experienced with a higher level of anxiety than what they actually experienced. That's the worst thing."

"But this is different. It was like a way of letting off steam, an ultra-violent fantasy. As if he wanted revenge for everything he's been through. Don't you think it's disturbing?"

"On the contrary, I think it's a good sign. It means he's moving beyond the trauma phase."

Mohammad spends the next two days in bed. His splitting headache is back, and he can't muster the strength to get up. My mother suggests they take a walk in the neighborhood, have coffee on a terrace or go see a movie. He turns her down each time. Instead, she nurses him with aspirin, peels apples to give him vitamins, prepares detox herbal teas, and brings him meals in bed. Each time, he thanks her half-heartedly.

Marie-France is puzzled. Why doesn't he make an effort? Why is he so apathetic? Perhaps he's a hypochondriac? Or else lazy? Was this all a mistake?

After 48 hours, she decides to call Michel, our family doctor who looked after us for years. He was at my father's side until the end. He's sure to be able to get Mohammad back on his feet. Michel examines him but can't find anything wrong. He takes my mother aside into the kitchen and announces his conclusion: Mohammad is in a state of shock. The change of environment has been too abrupt, and he needs time to adjust. My mother is disconcerted. She thought this house could only do him good, and it's having the opposite effect. Not to mention, he's supposed to start working soon. But the doctor is firm: he needs rest. She'll have to be patient. Not an easy task for my mother.

She fixes a cup of tea and a brioche and takes a tray up to Mohammad. "I'm really sorry," he apologizes. "I should be the happiest man on earth."

My mother redirects her worry and frustration to material details. Mohammad can't possibly have enough clothes in his little suitcase. She makes a series of phone calls to find him a job, insisting that he can't wind up washing dishes or working in the warehouse of some clothing shop. He needs to be in contact with people, to prod him out of his shell. She finally lands him a position as a salesclerk in the concept store—a shop with the carefully curated and unique selection of products—she created a few years ago with my father. She now must make sure Mohammad is presentable.

She calls up my brother Thomas, who lives next door, and asks him to bring over some of the things he no longer wears.

An hour later, he turns up with a bag full of good looking trousers, brandname shirts, and a gorgeous cashmere coat. He's accompanied by his three children, excited to meet Mohammad. They have made drawings for him. My mother sends a text to ask him to come down to meet her son and grandchildren. When he shows up a few minutes later in the living room, my mother immediately realizes it's a mistake. The children stand clutching their drawings, staring at him like a circus animal. He puts on a brave face and thanks them kindly, but she can tell he's uneasy. It suddenly hits her how humiliating it must be. She cuts the visit short, thanks Thomas, and ushers them out the door. The children don't get it. She asks my brother to explain.

She returns to the living room where Mohammad stands holding the bag of clothes. He thanks her then retreats to his room.

He lies back down and tries to gather his wits. He hates himself for being incapable of showing more gratitude. All those years of uncertainty, wandering, tension, and violence have wrung him dry. He can't muster any compassion, empathy or the least altruism. How can someone give love when they feel no love for themselves?

He's spent so much time merely trying to subsist from one day to the next, he's forgotten how to interact with people. He's going to have to get back on track if he wants any hope of assimilating. He knows it's going to take time. He hopes Marie-France will be patient.

need to talk to my mother. Get a better idea of what's going on over by the Invalides and put my mind at ease. Who is this guy living in my parents' home?

I call her. She's finishing lunch alone in the kitchen. The weather is nice. She's got the windows open to enjoy the mild November day. Over the phone I can hear birds chirping in the garden.

She tells me Mohammad has spent the past two days in bed, but she's managed to convince him to come out with her to a restaurant that night. She intends to get him back on his feet. "I've found him a job. He's got to be up for it."

Why is she doing all this? I've always seen her incredible generosity to be a blend of goodness and guilt. Goodness inherited from her mother, who was a saint; and guilt at being alive, unlike four of her sisters who died prematurely from cancer; at being richer than most of her friends; and at having recognition without really seeking it.

"I'm naive, I know what I'm doing is negligible in terms of poverty on a global scale, but for Mohammad, it's huge. It all boils down to a question of perspective."

"Don't you think you're doing this out of guilt?"

"Oh, no! How dreadful!"

"Why? Guilt isn't necessarily negative. People do lots of amazing things out of guilt. When I give money to a homeless person in the street, it's driven by generosity, of course; but, also, because I feel guilty for being born on the right side of the tracks and having such better luck than him in life. There's no shame in that."

"I don't like that idea."

Despite the cool autumn air, my mother suggests they walk to the small Afghan restaurant behind the Pantheon she discovered. She spent hours online looking for a good place. She read reviews, checked out photos, studied the menu. She figured he would enjoy reconnecting with his roots. When they walk in, they're greeted by a savory aroma. Mohammad freezes before a huge photo of snow-capped mountains: the exact same ones he saw from his bedroom window in his parents' house. Traditional kilim rugs hang on the walls, replicas of the ones on the floors in the family home in Isfahan. My mother senses his emotion and tries to put him at ease.

"Would you like to be near the kitchen or in the dining area?"

"By the window."

He sits with his back to the landscape of his childhood. Mohammad opens the menu. He struggles to keep his emotions in check. He chooses an *ashak* for a starter and *qabuli* for his entrée.

"You need to earn a living. I'm convinced you can do much better than the sales position I'm offering you, but it's already an opportunity. When I was your age, I was an au pair girl in England, but it didn't stop me from realizing my dreams. On the contrary, it strengthened me. You need to make money. Whether we like it or not, money means freedom."

Mohammad peers at her.

"I'm also going to lend you a few hundred euros that you can pay back out of your first paychecks. You need to have the means to go out. You can't lie around in your room all the time. I know my home is comfortable, but you need to meet people your own age. It's the only way to improve your French and assimilate." She pours two glasses of wine.

"Thank you, Marie-France."

The waiter brings a dish of lamb dumplings smothered in a sauce of chickpeas, cilantro and yogurt. My mother, still on her perpetual diet, makes do with a salad of eggplant and sweet peppers.

Mohammad takes a bite and sets his fork down.

"How is it? Do you like it?"

"Very much. This is the first time I've had Afghan food since I left Afghanistan. It's been a long journey, it's been ages since I've seen those mountains, walked on these rugs, smelled cumin or tasted *ashak*. It's stirring up a lot of memories. It's nice, but painful at the same time."

"Have you met any other Afghans since you arrived in Paris?"

"A few. I can tell just by listening to them whether they have an open mind, regardless of what they say. The things that bothered me there bother me even more here. Some of them have traveled thousands of miles, but deep down they haven't changed a bit. They're the ones I avoid. The others, I enjoy seeing from time to time. There's a group of Iranians that get together regularly. They are well-read and broad-minded. I like them."

He finishes his meal in silence then looks up. "Do you ever feel like you want to die?"

"No. Why? Do you?"

"Often."

Once they've finished, my mother excuses herself to go to the ladies' room. On her way, she asks the waiter if the owner could come to their table. A few minutes later, a charming woman in her sixties with a headscarf appears. After introductions, the discussion shifts into Dari. My mother can't understand a word, but the spark in Mohammad's eyes isn't lost on her.

He thanks her as they leave. Though he loved tasting his country's food once more, he admits he'd rather go to French restaurants in the future. Message received.

They take a taxi home. My mother is pensive as Mohammad watches the city stream past the window. She's used to being in control, trusting her instincts, having a good understanding of those around her. Her relationships are simple and transparent, and she interacts easily with others, but she's not sure how to behave with Mohammad. She gets the impression she makes him feel uncomfortable, that she offends him, that she's always missing the mark. The feeling is new for her.

• • •

Mohammad stops outside a fancy building situated in the 5th *arrondissement*. To the right of the double doors, above the keypad, a gilded plaque reads: *Doctor Richard Rechtman—Psychiatrist/Psychoanalyst*. He goes up to the fifth floor and takes a seat in a small waiting room. Out the window, he sees the dome of the Val-de-Grâce military hospital, symbol of the French army he was once proud to be part of but loathes today.

Richard calls him into his office and invites him to sit down. "Well?"

Mohammad talks about his origins, relates his journey and arrival at Marie-France's. "I'm very anxious. I think I'm depressed. It's normal in my case, with all I've been through. I lost everything, and I'm no longer in contact with my loved ones. But I know it's temporary. As soon as my life changes, I'll feel better. What worries me most is the splitting headache that won't go away. It's physical, but probably psychological, too. This is the first time I've ever been worried about my health."

Mohammad's voice drones on as if rattling off a speech learned by rote. He strives for accuracy and overanalyzes himself. The discussion has to lead to something concrete. He wants a solution right away.

"What makes you the saddest?"

"I'm not where I want to be. I'm alone. I want to study. I want to go to Sciences Po. That's my goal."

Richard nods.

"Do you have any advice?"

Richard smiles. "See you next week."

Mohammad shakes his hand and leaves.

He walks back to my mother's place. He needs to think. He's upset. That doctor is getting paid to help him. Why won't he answer any questions? It's not a game. They're not in some movie. This is real life. His life. Maybe to Richard, it's just one more story; but to Mohammad, it's crucial. He knows if he can manage to get into that school, everything will change. He won't be depressed anymore, he won't be sad or want to die anymore, and he won't need to see a therapist. He clings to this thought, this impossible dream.

• • •

For Halloween, my mother organizes a party at home with her grandchildren, my Uncle Ben, Aunt Dominique, and Mitty, her American friend. She invites Mohammad to join them. He declines but she insists; she's even bought him a magician's hat. Besides, it'll do him good to socialize a little. He reluctantly accepts.

A Tunisian couscous is served around the large table in the dining room. The kids, full of Halloween candy, barely touch it and disappear into the next room, leaving only the adults. Everyone laughs and proposes toasts. All the merriment gets on Mohammad's nerves. He clenches his jaw. My uncle opens another bottle of red wine and starts talking about his trip to Afghanistan in 1978, a few days before the war with the Soviets broke out. He describes the shepherds on the northern steppes, with their herds of 400 sheep; the *buzkashi* matches where men on horseback would compete to seize a decapitated goat carcass; the Bamiyan Valley, with its breathtaking giant Buddhas, destroyed by the Taliban thirteen years later; and Kabul, swarming with soldiers and tanks as it geared up for war. Mohammad likes hearing about his country. He thinks of his parents, the snowy streets of his neighborhood, the inner courtyard of his house, and the ruby pomegranate seeds he loved to pop in his mouth. On the other hand, he doesn't like the way people talk to him. They're too attentive or restrained or gentle. He sees pity and condescension in their eyes and it pains him. Even though he knows he's welcome in this family, he feels ill at ease.

My mother notices and suggests he get some rest. Freedom. He bids everyone goodnight and disappears.

She's angry with herself. Once again, she moved too fast.

When the guests have gone, she climbs the stone stairs and knocks on Mohammad's door.

"Yes?"

She finds him lying on his bed.

"I'm sorry."

"I'm the one who should be sorry."

"You know, I'm well aware it's easier to give than to receive."

When she's gone, he repeats the phrase over and over: "It's easier to give than to receive." Mohammad likes this kind of simple wisdom. He feels he's made a big step forward, each time he manages to put his feelings into words. He's been through hell and grown up too fast. There's so much he didn't have time to absorb. People see him as a young man, but he's already old. Like a cat, he's aged seven times faster than the humans around him.

My mother's friends rally around; the family, too. Alain gives Mohammad some CDs; Adrienne and Arnaud, a fridge; Christine, a chest of drawers; Thomas, several pairs of pants; Julien, shirts; Laurence cleans his teeth for free; Lena introduces him to her friends; Marie-Hélène does his laundry; Celine and Bernard give him French classes; Bernie and Sylvie hired him, and later on, so does Martine.

Some people probably figure my mother is easing her conscience at low cost; that with all the space she has, it's normal she should take in Mohammad. It's true, she's got room. But those who are most welcoming aren't necessarily the ones with the biggest homes. I read about one family who put four kids into one bedroom, so they could lodge a refugee in their small apartment. Then there's the single woman in a two-room apartment in the Paris suburbs. She couldn't stand the sight of people sleeping beneath her windows and now permanently houses one or two in her living room.

My mother has done what a lot of people would like to do, but don't. Talk is often a world away from action. I, too, thought about it when my daughter left for college; we had an empty room in our Brooklyn home. I realized I wasn't prepared to host someone in my house, to share my bathroom, kitchen and living room. I tell myself it's because I work at home and can't risk the distraction. But, in reality, I'm loathe to give up my comfort. Why, to our Western minds, is that concept so important? Why can't we manage to give it up? Why are we so focused on ourselves?

As soon as he's back on his feet, Mohammad finds himself at Merci, the concept store. He's struck by the average age of the exployees—all very young—and the elegance of the shop, the vast premises and stylish decor.

The manager has him sign a contract and gives him a position in sales. At first, he'll rotate through the different departments to familiarize himself with the spirit of the shop and what they offer: clothing, home furnishings, hardware, linens, a bookshop, a stationary shop, a café, and a restaurant. If everything goes well, once his French is better, he'll get a permanent position in the fashion department.

After a few days of work, he makes friends with Bernie. As manager of the Used Books Café on the ground floor, she suggests he come work with her. Hot drinks, quiches, tarts, and a vast array of used books. Mohammad feels immediately at home. He splits his time between working in the kitchen and out on the floor. It reminds him of the years he worked at the English Embassy or Sodexo. But everything's so much more luxurious here. Easier and more exciting.

A few days later, my mother invites him to breakfast before work. She explains the store manager phoned to tell her he's too slow. He needs to move faster, be quicker on his feet. Mohammad takes this in and promises to fix things.

In the subway on his way to work, he gives himself a silent pep talk. He's going to show them what he's capable of. He wants Marie-France to be proud of him.

As soon as he arrives, he sets to work and quickens the pace. The manager smiles. His efforts are clearly paying off.

Mohammad likes the people who come into the shop. They come from all over the world. They're chic, curious, cultivated, refined, and trendy. Occasionally, he has a flashback to how, just one month ago, he was homeless, humiliated, broken, and in despair. It makes his head spin.

Besides landing him a job, my mother offers to pay for night classes at the Alliance Française. Assimilation comes through language.

If Mohammad wants to study, make friends, and fall in love, mastering French is essential. His whole life, Mohammad has tried to grasp the subtleties of language. He's spent lots of time analyzing how people express themselves; what words one can use to be original without appearing crazy; what turns of phrase are funny; how to be serious when needed; ironic; mocking without being humiliating; manipulate grammar; use slang; vocabulary; a polished style. Now he must learn it all over again. He knows it won't happen in a day. Often people wonder why he says so little. They think he's strange, anti-social, impolite, maybe even dumb. It's painful.

The best way to thank my mother would be to work hard and be a diligent student. Unfortunately, Mohammad is exhausted from his workdays. He has less and less energy to attend a night class at the Alliance Française. He doesn't dare tell her. He tries to keep up but has trouble concentrating, often dozing off in class. When he's simply too tired, he plays hooky, sneaks home and hides up in his room, hoping she doesn't notice.

• • •

My mother thinks Mohammad needs some rest. She suggests he come along with her for a weekend in Recloses, where she's taking my brother's children.

While the kids play out in the yard, they sit by the fire sipping tea. She talks a lot; Mohammad still struggles with French.

He reminds her of the men and women she read about who returned from concentration camps at the end of World War II. He doesn't want to share. He wants to forget and move on. He feels humiliated at all the suffering he's been through, and he can't stand pity.

So, she talks about simple things. Her beliefs and convictions, valuable advice she's received throughout her life. He listens diligently, wishing he could write it all down. He thanks her. Her words appear to comfort him. Their conversation lasts until after sundown.

My mother has forgotten all about the kids, who must be on the trampoline way at the back of the yard. They'll sleep well tonight! Mohammad tells her he hasn't felt this good in years. Emotions he'd thought were lost are reawakening.

They haven't known each other very long, and yet my mother can tell he's more relaxed. Even though he still conceals many things, he's gradually starting to open up. She never forces him. She listens attentively and is never intrusive. She walks on eggshells. Day after day, meal after meal, movie after movie, he speaks more freely.

"No one's ever been so nice to me, except my mother."

He speaks about his mother and the deep connection they share. He confides about her hopelessness at his three brothers' horrible behavior. The eldest was heavily into drugs, and the other two were very macho and treated her disrespectfully. Mohammad often saw her cry and would console her. For as long as he can remember, he had always felt closer to his sisters and mother than to the men in his family. Mohammad's brothers would make fun of him. They'd grown up in a harsh society, in a poor family where you had to impose yourself to survive. They became men too early. They'd lost all sense of gentleness and were incapable of showing affection. Mohammad, on the other hand, was sweet. He loved his mother. She did everything around the house and never had a minute to herself. Mohammad would help whenever he could. He wanted to see his mom smile, and sometimes she would when it was just the two of them. But from an early age, he knew they'd be separated one day; that he'd leave home and go far away from the suffocating society they lived in. This made their time together even more precious. Mohammad savored every minute. When his mother would cook, he'd hang out in the kitchen making jokes. He loved to hear her laugh. He missed her every second of the day.

He calls her regularly by Skype. Not a month goes by that they don't talk. He tells her all about his new life and she listens attentively. He'd love to bring her to France one day, but he's not sure she could handle the trip. She's only 60, but people age a lot faster in Kabul than Paris.

Mohammad tells my mother how after he left Afghanistan, he would have a recurring dream. One of their cats was escaping and running into the middle of a busy street. It would get trapped amid the traffic rushing past. His mother would dash out to save it and get run over by a military truck.

It reminds my mother of the dream she kept having in the initial months after my father passed away. Night after night, he'd appear to her and announce he was leaving her for another woman.

My mother and I, also, have a close bond. When I left, it came as a shock. My mother's a homebody who's always lived in the same city. For years she spent every vacation in the same place—Provence in the summer, the mountains in winter. As such, she could never wrap her mind around my desire to live somewhere else, far away from her. She was sad I was leaving and thrown by my decision to become a cab driver. Then, when my first book *Yellow Cab* was published, she bought dozens of copies and gave them to all her friends. One day, I discovered a message she'd written on the flyleaf in one of them. (It's weird to see your mother has signed your own book. I took it as an act of love.) *Cherish our children's differences and the life that brings them happiness.* She'd nailed it.

When I left, it created a void she sought to fill, even though she firmly refutes the idea of replacing me. Obviously, I'm not the only one who left the fold. If my father were still around, Mohammad would undoubtedly have remained in his shelter out in the suburbs. The imbalance caused by his death gave my mother the strength, and desire, to welcome a stranger into her home.

It turns out the place I left in order to reinvent myself has become a refuge for Mohammad. He dreams of seeing his family again, whereas I needed to distance myself from mine to allow myself to live differently. I think of the French novelist Alice Zeniter's reflection on her grandfather's exile: *He wanted to live his own life, convinced that the warmth he'd lose by distancing himself from the herd would be compensated by the space and time solitude would bring him.* This is exactly what I've felt since my own departure. And in the end, even though he suffers from having had no choice, Mohammad's life will certainly be richer than if he had stayed near his herd.

Mohammad often talks to me about the pain caused by separation. I try to reassure him. Time and distance allow us to build a different sort of bond. I explain how my relationship with my mother has deepened since I left France. Perhaps in the same way, his own connection to his mother will be stronger when he sees her again. He stares at me and gives a little nod. I can tell he's puzzled. Our realities are light years apart. I can hop on a plane any time I want and go hug my mother. He can't.

The next day, as they're about to head back to Paris, early in the afternoon to avoid the Sunday traffic jams, Mohammad tells my mother, "This is the most beautiful house I've ever seen."

"We can have your wedding here, if you like."

Mohammad wants to get back into music. He hasn't composed anything since he left Afghanistan. The rap songs he recorded in his native tongue rely mainly on lyrics; it would be hard to play them for professionals in Paris. He's going to talk to my mother about it. She knows a lot of people; she must have some connections in the field.

He goes down to the kitchen. She's eating dinner alone. Grilled steak and green beans. She invites him to sit and opens a bottle of wine. They clink glasses. Mohammad tells her about his idea. For him, music is a yelp of anger. He pours everything he's unable to express on a daily basis into it. When he was a teenager in Afghanistan, hip-hop kept him from going crazy. It was how he let off steam. He pulls a photo from his wallet of himself and two friends in the hills of Kabul. All three of them are striking the typical poses of American rappers. Mohammad sports a skull and crossbones bandana on his head, a Lakers' jersey, a gold chain with military dog tags, dark-blue baggy pants, and worn Adidas sneakers. He tells her if he could start composing and playing again, he'd surely feel less alone.

My mother admits she has about as many connections in the rap world as among rice growers in China. She racks her brain but can only come up with NTM and IAM. French groups her sons listened to back in the 20th century. Are they still making music? Are they still even alive? She's disconcerted at her total lack of knowledge in the field. She can't see herself tootling off in her SmartCar to meet figures from the new French hip-hop scene. She scours her address book for some forgotten contact who could come to the rescue. She has connections in fashion, media, and the restaurant business; but nothing in the music industry. The only thing she can think of is a dentist friend with several patients who work in show buisness. My mother calls her up. She's onboard and immediately names a few music artists my mother's never heard of. Then she offers to organize a gathering, asap, with whoever among them is free. She's excited by the prospect of helping Mohammad.

• • •

My mother sets the table in the dining room, typically reserved for holiday dinners. Meals are usually eaten in the kitchen. She brings out the silver, builds a fire in the fireplace, and lights candles in the living room. Mohammad, dressed to kill, helps her fix plates with carrot sticks, parmesan shavings, grilled almonds, spicy green olives, thin slices of pickled black radish, and multicolored cherry tomatoes on an antique wooden tray. At our home, the *apéritif*—a key moment of the evening—has always been generous, like a Tunisian *kemia*.

The guests arrive. My mother makes the introductions. Mohammad, Alain Chamfort. Alain, Mohammad.

The singer is accompanied by Laurence, the dentist friend, and Bernard, a 60-something music producer who worked with Gilbert Montagnier, Serge Lama, and other French has-beens from the 1980s. Mohammad has never heard of any of them, but quickly realizes, given the average age of the guests, they have nothing to do with the hip-hop scene. Everyone's kindness makes up for his disappointment. The singer warmly invites him to come to his studio. Mohammad is thrilled. They fix a date for the following week. The producer admits he's "left all that behind," but offers to give Mohammad French classes. He graduated from Sciences Po and used to teach before getting into music. He suggests they study Saint-Exupéry's *The Little Prince*. As for Laurence, she offers to open her address book to him if he needs more contacts. Everyone leaves, "delighted to have met."

The next week, Mohammad visits Chamfort in his studio, a luxurious padded room with exotic wood, thick velvet, and leather chairs. They settle onto the comfy sofa to talk. Chamfort is curious and wants to know more about Mohammad's music. He asks about his projects and ambitions. Mohammad shows him videos of Afghan rappers and plays some of his songs for him. Chamfort seems enthusiastic. How about they try recording something together next time?

In the following months, Mohammad tries to reach Chamfort many times. No luck. Has he gone on tour? Changed his number? Or simply no longer wants to see him? Does he find Mohammad's music mediocre? Maybe Chamfort's right. The amateur tracks he recorded in a Kabul basement are certainly not polished enough.

Mohammad hears the wind whistling through the shutters and

stares out his window at clouds scuttling across the sky. On his nightstand is the book that changed his life. The copy his friend Naïm gave him back in the kitchen of the British Embassy. He's kept it with him ever since. He picks it up and leafs through to page 146. *Think 'How?' instead of 'Why?'* He rereads the chapter for the umpteenth time. *When faced with unpleasant events, unsuccessful people tend to complain, constantly asking, 'Why? Why did this disaster happen to me? Why am I so unfortunate? Why am I always a failure? Why?' When you think in terms of 'why,' you unknowingly destroy your spirit, and your subconscious hits a dead end. Not only does it accept failure, but it also makes no effort to solve the problem. In contrast, successful, happy people constantly ask themselves, 'How? How can I best solve my problems? How can I achieve my goal? How can I design a wonderful future for myself? How?'*

Mohammad closes the book. He lies back on his bed and thinks. How can Chamfort's silence be beneficial to him? What lesson can he learn from it? Perhaps it's a sign. Maybe it's time to focus on his education. He can always pick up music again later. With the knowledge, experience, and maturity he'll accumulate in the years to come, his lyrics will only be richer and his music, more intense. He imagines one day using music to reach his fellow Afghans. A political, anti-establishment rap that will open their eyes and change their world.

make a quick trip to France for a friend's wedding. The yellow cab driver who takes me to JFK is named Mohammad, too. He's also from Kabul. I tell him about the encounter between my mother and his namesake.

"Every Afghan who's left their country has a special story." He proceeds to tell me his:

His parents were both high school teachers, until the Taliban took power and banned his mother from working. Shortly after, they killed his father and brother-in-law. Mohammad was 15. His mother found herself alone with seven children. An aunt who lived in Los Angeles told her about a program the First Lady Hillary Clinton had just created, to welcome Afghan widows on American soil. She went to the embassy to tell her story and was granted political asylum for the whole family. They arrived in New York in 2001, a few days before 9/11. In the following months, Mohammad, who worked at a Halal grocery shop in Harlem, received several threats. A group of tough-looking guys would come into his shop every day to tell him they were going to have his hide. One day, a group of African Americans from the neighborhood stopped in. Their leader, a former drug dealer who'd become an imam in the main mosque in the north of the city, had heard about the threats some of the neighborhood shopkeepers were getting and wanted to make sure there were no problems. Mohammad explained the situation. They came back the next day as the insults were flying. The imam grabbed the group's leader and smashed his head into the wall. When the guy turned around and realized who he was dealing with, he dropped to his knees, begged to be spared and promised never to bother any Muslims again.

As soon as I reach Paris, I call (our) Mohammad.

We meet at the Rosebud. Dim lighting, excellent cocktails and New Orleans jazz. Mohammad tells me the music is "killing" him. "Here I am, drinking an Old Fashioned with a friend. I feel happy."

"Do you ever regret leaving Afghanistan?"

"If I'd stayed, I'd probably be dead by now. But if I were still alive, I probably would have worked for other foreign forces—the British or Americans. I would have saved up and continued helping my family. As soon as I'd put enough aside, I would have gone back to music and studied political science. Ten years later, I would have had a wife, kids and a house. That was my dream. But the reality was a lot more complex. I had few contacts. I was different. My way of thinking didn't correspond to the world around me. I had to pretend. If my parents asked me to pray or observe Ramadan, I had no choice but to comply. Because, even if I no longer believed in God, I believed in love. I didn't want to hurt them. Even today, when they call and ask if I've said my prayers, I lie. Life is simple for people who are content to get up every day, follow the rules, and pray. Sometimes it makes me jealous. When you drink a glass of water, it's wonderful not to think about why; you fill your glass with cool water, you drink it, and you feel good. But once you start asking yourself, 'Why am I drinking water?' then everything gets complicated. Today I think of my life as sitting on a scale. On one side are all the negative elements. Everything I experienced during my first 20 years. And on the other, the positive things I have accumulated since I came here. The scales are still tipped way over to the bad side, but I can tell they're gradually starting to balance out. Maybe one day they'll tip to the other side."

"You know, Mohammad, this may sound shocking but, in light of your capacities, it's lucky you made it here. It may have been unspeakably brutal, but it's also an incredible opportunity. Now you live in a free country, and will be able to realize the exceptional potential you have. You're going to do amazing things."

"You're my friend, so I'll allow you to shake me up a bit."

I tell him about my French teacher back in high school who told a student in my class that she was lucky after her father just passed away. "Look around at your classmates with their little middle-class lives. They're dry, they've got nothing to tell, nothing to revolt against. Everything's so easy, it makes you want to die of boredom." At the time, I was disgusted; shocked by his lack of sensitivity. But today, I understand. I explain to Mohammad that although he'll certainly have to grapple with more obstacles than people who lock themselves away in comfort and ignorance, he'll wind up going further. And the day he finally achieves happiness, it'll be so much greater.

I speak to Mohammad like a big brother. For the first time. "It's like love. When you fall in love, you run the risk of suffering terribly the day it ends, and unfortunately it always comes to an end at some point, one way or another, but it's worth it. The only time in your life you're not aware of this is when you're a child."

"I didn't really have any childhood. I grew up as an adult. The violence and trauma I experienced were a double-edged sword. On the one hand, they made me stronger; but on the other, they destroyed a lot of things inside."

"Do you feel like the things that were destroyed can be rebuilt? Or does the damage feel irreversible?"

"I don't know."

"Maybe talking to someone could help you come to terms with what's weighing on you, so you can move forward."

Mohammad takes a long sip of whisky and pops the maraschino cherry floating among the ice cubes into his mouth. "Depends on who. Talking to you, for instance, is helpful."

"Maybe you should talk to a professional."

"I've been seeing your mother's psychiatrist friend Richard for the last two months."

• • •

I invite Richard to dinner.

We meet in a restaurant near the Bastille. He asks about my life in New York and wonders how my mother is dealing with the new situation. I explain how the family has readjusted since my departure. My mother has become closer to my two brothers, and our relationship has grown stronger. I steer the discussion to Mohammad. Richard immediately warns me that, as a professional, he's sworn to secrecy and can't reveal anything personal.

I tell him about our long discussions by the fire. "I feel like it's good for him. There aren't a lot of people he can talk to. His French isn't strong enough to hold a discussion yet, and he refuses to meet other Afghans."

"He needs to break with the past. With his origins, his name: a way to put it all behind him and make a fresh start. I tell him how this reminds me of my father who cut off all ties after he left Tunisia in the early 1960s.

"What migrants experience today is even worse. They're chased from their homeland, they risk their lives and when they arrive here, they get rejected. I'm sure it was hard for your father to be uprooted, but the reality of immigration is much more hostile today than 50 years ago. Or even as recently as the 1980s, for example, with the boat people, whose experience was equally traumatic. They received a warm welcome when they arrived in France. That changes everything. Culturally speaking, Syrians, Iraqis and Afghans are much closer to us than Cambodians and Vietnamese. People who abandon everything and take major risks to leave their countries have basically chosen to be in charge of their own death. In other words, rather than be killed by bombs or get murdered, they die at sea, on the beach or in the mountains, but it's their choice. It's a subjective rescue. The problem is, when they arrive, they figure they're safe, and the urgency of survival diminishes. They're no longer in a situation of life or death; instead, they're left with social death and a shitty life. And they weren't expecting that. When you're up against such a monumental challenge, you tell yourself that if you survive, no matter what happens next will inevitably be good. Whereas on the contrary, they experience humiliation on a daily basis. They're treated as nobodies. It's horrendous. Especially for those who are educated and had a certain social standing. The disconnect is overwhelming. Their experience is equivalent to the pogroms against Jews in Eastern Europe in the 1930s. My Polish grandfather was 13 when he left Warsaw during World War I. All on his own, he walked across war-torn Europe, hoping to finally make it to the U.S., but he ended up stopping in France. At the time, Jews were beaten in the streets and treated as scapegoats. Despite that, and the fact he only spoke Yiddish, he was able to make a fortune. But when the Nazis came, he lost everything. Generation after generation of persecution creates strong subjective positions. It's often been said that Jews were the most powerful intellectuals in the 20th century because they were persecuted. You're forced to free yourself from the constraints of a closed space, and open up to the world, in spite of everything. For example, Afghanistan with its clans—which Mohammad fled from—is horrendous. It's a blessing he managed to get out."

I try to imagine Richard's sessions with Mohammad. Does he explain all this? Does he ask Mohammad about his past? Or does he just let him talk? And does Mohammad tell the truth?

"You have to remember these people have both a collective fate—because they're all caught up in the same history—and a multitude of individual stories. The problem is, we tend to saddle them with a global label that is extremely hard to wear. They're 'Afghans,' 'Syrians,' 'Kurds,' 'migrants.' For them, it's very unsettling. That's why it's amusing when Mohammad asks you what you would do if you were an Afghan refugee, when the real question is, 'What would you do if you were me?' "

Richard pauses for another sip of wine. I wonder how this man, who's fought for over 30 years to help martyrized populations, can still keep the faith.

"I'm touched by the way your mother talks about Mohammad. She speaks about him very naturally, like one of your brothers or any other family friend. It's uncommon, and it's laudable not to have turned him into a representative of the 'other.' It's probably one of the reasons Mohammad feels so comfortable with her. In fact, he told me she was the first person he's completely trusted since he left Afghanistan. The way she sees him must play a big role. We don't realize just how important trust is for people in his situation. We use the word 'trust' so often it's become a bit trite, but it's a fundamental term. We don't think about it, but our entire society is based on trust. For instance, right here in this restaurant, unconsciously, you trust everyone. You don't imagine someone is going to burst through the door with an AK-47; you're not worried the guy behind you is going to leap up and slit your throat; you don't wonder if someone has poisoned the wine, and so on. It's an extremely complex psychological operation. It means you trust your environment. You feel safe. When you lose this mechanism, you're paralyzed, because you can't delegate anything. You can't trust anyone other than yourself. How do you live? How do you sleep? You lock yourself up inside. And if you have to sleep with someone, how do you manage that? These people have constant nightmares. Some even go mad. So, if your mother has restored his sense of trust, that's an amazing thing."

"Are you optimistic?"

"Mohammad truly has a great deal of charisma. If we manage to pull him out of his depression, he's got everything he needs to shine."

The dinner is winding up. I excuse myself to go to the restroom. In the toilet bowl, I spot a fly flailing in the water. I hesitate, pee on it and flush.

My plane is at 11:45 am. My mother and I have time for one last breakfast together before I head to the airport.

She asks me about Mohammad, whom she hasn't seen much of the past few days. She's happy about the friendship we're developing. For months, she was his only connection. Today he knows he can count on me, even if I live far away. Every time I come back to Paris, we see each other. Of course, I'm gathering material for my project, but I realize more and more I enjoy spending time with him. We're both impatient for the day he'll finally be able to visit New York.

My mother's in a talkative mood. She says now that she's gotten to know Mohammad better, she realizes she had a simplistic interpretation of why he was unhappy. She assumed it was linked to what he'd been through before he met her. Persecution, homelessness, nights in the street, hunger, and above all, humiliation. She thought someone who'd escaped from hell and the precarity he'd been through and landed in a place like hers, was bound to be happy. Instantaneously. While, in fact, he's like an alien dropped into a world he knows nothing about. One day, he admitted he felt like he was seven instead of 20. That his real birth was the day he discovered *Think Yourself Successful* and began thinking for himself. My mother realizes that besides giving him a roof over his head, she must look after him like a child. It's not enough to do his laundry; feed him; find him work. She must also be attentive; listen to him; advise him; reassure him; converse for hours; take him out for meals; invite him to the theater; and lecture him from time to time. When he first came into her life, she assumed she'd give him a nice place to live and a job, and that would be enough. And besides, she figured he probably didn't want an old lady on his back. She was wrong.

• • •

Mohammad buys a cactus.

He's inspired by its strength, solidity, longevity, capacity for survival in an arid environment, and its slow, inexorable growth.

He's been spending most of his free time meditating. Trying to find his path. He finally has a secure place to live and must now think about what comes next. How to use this opportunity to go even further, to excel and surpass himself. But he still has trouble concentrating. His brain is foggy. Meditation helps free his mind from parasitic thoughts about the past, and to focus on the future. He practices a lot and can tell he's making progress.

His only concern is that my mother won't understand why he's locking himself up in his room again. He doesn't want her to think he's surfing the Internet when he's sitting quietly before his cactus.

She's a rational woman. The concept of meditation most likely escapes her.

When Mohammad tells me about his cactus, my eyes light up. I, too, have a passion for succulents: the way they're anatomically distinct from other plants; the way their felt-like structure resembles a pin cushion with spines, hair, branches or even flowers depending on the season; the way they range in size from tiny spheres less than an inch in diameter, to 60-foot-tall trees that weigh 25 tons. My first real encounter with cacti was in Tuscon, Arizona, a few years back. At the time, I was developing a movie about two brothers looking for their mother in the middle of the desert. I was immediately fascinated by this city encircled by cacti just a few miles from the Mexican border. Ever since, I go back regularly. Each time, I stay at the Hotel Congress, a historic late-19th century building above a concert venue. The receptionist hands out earplugs when you check in. A sign over the counter reads, *We're a noisy hotel. We do not give discounts due to noise. What do you expect? It's rock'n'roll.* For nightlife, guests can choose between various bands playing in the legendary club, the three bars serving up amazing margaritas made with local tequila, and the outdoor restaurant featuring meat that's been smoked since dawn in a rusty barbecue shaped like a locomotive. The temperature never drops below 75°. Such close proximity to the desert gives the town a very particular feel. Driving through scenery that looks straight out of a John Ford Western, you expect to see a family of illegal immigrants jump out from behind a cactus at any second. The constant to-and-fro of border patrol vehicles on the deserted highways is a reminder of the merciless fight against immigration. Tuscon is the only Democratic city in an ultra-conservative state. Several associations are dedicated to helping illegal immigrants, and the locals join in by offering protection to the men and women who risk their lives crossing the desert—a source of fascination to tourists like myself, and of danger for them and their families. Even the local police sometimes refuse to help the border patrol.

Mohammad listens to me describe this faraway land with stars in his eyes. The chimerical draw of America.

After meditating and reflecting for several days, Mohammad decides to take up a challenge and try the impossible. Surpass and transcend himself. Surprise the whole world. Marie-France, his co-workers, his boss, the director of the shelter, the two Marcs—one from Colombo, one from Sarrebourg—the people back home, his parents, brothers, sisters, friends, Rohullah, Naïm, Jawad and Bagher. He's decided to take the next entrance exam to Sciences Po.

Mohammad can't continue earning a living as a waiter. He's come too far to settle for that, even if it is in the top concept store in Paris. He's ambitious and motivated. He would like to go to school. Most people work to make others' dreams possible; he wants to realize his own.

He's saved enough for the foreseeable future. He has no expenses, no rent, a free public transport pass, and eats most of his meals at work.

His only real spending is the money he sends to his parents. Every month, he gives them a third of what he earns. And sometimes there are unforeseen expenses. For example, his brother phoned a few weeks ago to announce he wanted to get married but didn't have enough money for the wedding. Since their parents are too old to work and couldn't help, he had to call it off. Without batting an eye, Mohammad gave him half his savings. He knew it would make his parents happy, and he couldn't stand the thought of them feeling sadder than they already were. So, he paid for the festivities he was unable to attend.

After years of living with nothing, he also treats himself occasionally. Mainly clothes. He wants to look neat and elegant, to blend into the world he's now part of. He's always had a taste for fashion. In Kabul, he would frequent a shop that sold secondhand designer brands. Not knock-offs made in China, but the real thing. It was important to him. Today he can afford brand new shirts and pants. It's better. He likes the way they smell.

After all he's been through, he feels he deserves a few indulgences.

Mohammad knows if he enrolls in college now, it will take him at least seven years to get the degree he dreams of. He's over 20. Is he too old to embark on such a challenge?

He makes a list. On one side, he writes the obstacles, risks and disadvantages. On the other, the possibilities and benefits. The verdict is in: 14 pros to eight cons. That decides it. He's going to focus on history, political science and management. He looks online for different preparatory classes he could apply to. He sends emails, makes phone calls, asks questions, gathers brochures, and visits dozens of schools. Not a single site or platform gives any information about what steps one should take to apply. It's a painstaking process that has, no doubt, discouraged more than one hopeful student. All the better, he thinks. Less competition. He starts hanging out at the Sorbonne. Though he's not enrolled in classes, he loves the atmosphere of the old university. The thrill of walking through the halls of an emblematic institution renowned among scholars all over the world. He talks to students and professors during their coffee breaks. One of them tells him about the recent creation of Wintegreat, an organization that helps refugees gain access to education and vocational training and put them on a career path. Why doesn't Mohammad contact them?

The very next day, Mohammad phones the association and learns he is eligible to turn in an application. They give him an appointment for the following week.

• • •

It's time to talk to Marie-France.

He invites her out to a little neighborhood bistro where she's a regular. She often comes to savor delicious steak tartare and salad, while secretly dreaming of blood sausage and mashed potatoes, the house specialty.

They leave the building, cross the avenue, and sit at the small table near the door.

Mohammad's known my mother for three months, and he's still just as impressed by her elegance, no matter the occasion. Tonight, she's wearing a long Japanese tunic and blue silk pants, perfectly polished oxfords, light makeup, and a fake ivory comb stuck jauntily in her grey hair.

"So, what's the occasion?" my mother teases him.

"Marie-France, I could invite you out every day, and it still wouldn't be enough to thank you for all you've done for me."

"Your presence, your courage and intelligence are thanks enough. It's a gift to have you in my home."

Mohammad lowers his gaze, takes a deep breath and musters his courage. He looks up and announces he's decided to give up his job as a server to prepare for the entrance exam for Sciences Po. My mother doesn't get it. She gently tries to explain just what a risk this is. He didn't go to high school, doesn't speak French very well, is no longer 18, and needs to earn a living. If he fails, which is not hard to imagine, his disappointment will be immense, and he'll probably plummet back into a depression.

"Most people who take this sort of exam have already spent years preparing for it and are often supported financially by their families. I'm all for being ambitious, but you must be careful not to set your sights too high. You could burn your wings, and believe me, that's extremely painful."

Usually Mohammad appreciates her advice, but not this time. "Trust me, I'm going to succeed. If I don't try now, I'll regret it for the rest of my life."

"I trust you completely, but I think you should be more realistic. Arrange things so you can keep your job while you prepare for the exam. If it doesn't work out, you'll be able to land on your feet." She pauses then adds, "Don't forget, your parents are counting on you."

Mohammad peers at her in silence. She smiles and reaches for his hand. "Let me make you an offer."

In the 1970s, my parents successfully founded a children's clothing brand. For them, it was the story of a lifetime. When they sold it 30 years later, they had enough money to live comfortably for the rest of their lives. They could have retired to a house by the sea in Italy, but they chose to stay and embark on a new challenge: they founded a new sort of concept store where all proceeds would go to an endowment fund benefiting children in Madagascar, the island nation in the Indian Ocean. For decades, Malagasy women made smocked dresses that were a pillar of success of my parents' previous business. Years later, they enjoyed being able to give back what they'd received. It was an immediate success, and the business grew quickly.

Shortly after my father fell ill, my mother didn't have the energy to carry on managing it alone, so she passed the torch. But she continued brimming over with ideas and projects: a children's clothing line for a Japanese label; a traditional French restaurant with old-fashioned decor; an upscale design and hardware store (in honor of my father); an online brand of tableware and household linens; and a style agency that made use of all her talents. Then a small tea room near her home was for sale. She bought it, redecorated it, and christened it Miss Marple. Now she offers to put Mohammad in charge of running it, alongside Martine, my father's sister, her partner in the business.

"The neighborhood clientele is obviously less exciting than in the concept store, but it won't be as tiring as commuting across town every day. And you'll have a position of real responsibility. How does that sound?"

Mohammad nods half-heartedly. He can hardly say no to her. Marie-France has decided to hand him the reins of her business. It's a remarkable show of trust. He's well aware of that. He's simply going to have to make it work.

My mother is delighted. She's sure he's the perfect fit for this new venture. She figures that if he likes it, perhaps his college obsession will pass.

At the end of the meal, the waiter brings the check. My mother automatically reaches for her wallet. "No, Marie-France. You're my guest tonight."

. . .

Mohammad sits in a small office across from a young woman named Marguerite. She explains how Wintegreat was founded in 2015 by Theo and Eymeric, two students at ESCP, a selective business school in Paris, who were concerned about the Syrian refugee crisis. Rather than succumb to the ambient miserabilism, they developed an integration program for new arrivals.

"To participate in the program, you have to be motivated and prepared to aim high. You need ambition, and an objective we can help you formulate. Our goal is to get you to dream big, so you don't settle for the first odd job that comes your way. In the first year, we had a variety of profiles—doctors, artists, journalists—who ranged from 18 to 46 years of age. Some had high school diplomas and wanted to continue their studies; others, after 15 years of work experience in their countries, wanted to reconnect professionally in France."

Her cell phone on the desk vibrates. She glances at the screen and turns it off. "Sorry. Let's start by having you fill out a questionnaire, so we can see if you meet all the requirements. If so, we'll call you in for an interview to evaluate your ambition, availability and motivation."

"I'm very motivated."

"That's a good start. Our program lasts six months. Unfortunately, we can only take 25 participants per semester."

Mohammad nods.

"After the interview, if you're selected, you'll benefit from highly-personalized assistance. You'll be paired up with a mentor who will help outline your project in detail and support you throughout the program. You'll also work with a student coach to implement the project. He or she will follow your progress daily, and also assist you with administration, if you have questions or run into any problems. On the other hand, you must understand that even if you get into our program, it won't give you special access to Sciences Po or any other school. You'll have to follow the standard application process, which is highly selective."

Marguerite's phone buzzes again. An emergency. She excuses herself and steps out into the hallway.

Only 25 spots for hundreds of applicants. And even if Mohammad does get in, he'll have a hard road ahead. Nevertheless, he has faith his luck will hold. He can't help picturing the day when he picks up the phone to announce to his mother, sitting at the kitchen table in their home in Dash-te Barchi, that he got into Sciences Po.

Marguerite comes back, apologizes, and hands Mohammad the application. They look it over briefly together, then she suggests he take his time filling it out at home. He needs to turn it in before Christmas. The candidates selected will be announced mid-January, and the interviews set up right afterwards. She wishes him Happy Holidays and hands him her card.

As soon as Mohammad gets back to his room, he sits at his desk and fills out the form. He reads it over carefully, slips it into a large envelope, and heads to the nearest post office. No time to lose.

• • •

Mohammad phones to tell me he sent his application to Wintegreat, then headed straight to City Hall to apply for French nationality. "I'm on a roll."

"Fingers crossed. Are you impatient to be French?"

"I can't wait to be able to travel freely. You know, there's nowhere I feel at home. I'm like a child who's lost his mother. Wherever I go, I'll meet nice people who are kind and encouraging, but they'll never replace my mother. My experience has taught me that I don't belong to any country. My only home is my family. And I'm not allowed to see them anymore."

For now, Mohammad has political refugee status, which is valid for ten years. This gives him the right to live and work in France, and it means he can travel within the Schengen Area—26 European states that abolished passports for travel within their mutual borders—but he can't return to Afghanistan. The last time he saw his parents was four years ago.

To obtain French nationality, one must prove they have a place to live, a job, and can speak French. Mohammad has already taken the language proficiency test. He scored a B1. High enough to apply. There's no reason his request should be denied.

He gathers his pay slips, fills out a form he downloaded from the ministry's website, asks my mother for proof of lodging and an electricity bill, then makes an appointment at City Hall. He waits three hours in line just to file his application.

His new nationality will be the opportunity for him to change his name. He wants to get rid of the first part and simply go by Med. He's keen to drop the letters that represent suffering, religion and ignorance. Erase the past and make a break from the first part of his life. Become someone else.

As soon as he gets his new passport, he plans to go see his parents. He misses them terribly, even if they get to Skype every other week.

I remind Mohammad that if he wants to visit me in the U.S., finally discover New York, fly to Tucson or see his friend Bagher, who finally got a visa and now drives a taxi in Austin, Texas, he'll have to plan the trip before he goes back to visit his family. Once he's got an Afghan stamp in his passport, it won't be easy to enter the U.S., especially if Trump is still in office.

After logging Mohammad's application into the computer, the passport officer says he should get a reply in one to two years.

He's got plenty of time to think about it.

I t's the grand opening at Miss Marple. Marie-France's friends are there, as well as a handful of journalists. Mohammad makes the rounds of guests, serving wine and thin slices of olive cake. Everyone congratulates my mother for her talent as a decorator. Leopard carpeting, deep benches with colorful velvet cushions, old-fashioned chandeliers, black-framed animal engravings, marble countertops and white tablecloths.

The very next day, the establishment is filled with neighborhood locals, curious customers, and trendy Parisians who've already read articles on the Internet.

It doesn't take long for Mohammad to realize he won't be happy there. Nevertheless, he continues serving scones, soft boiled eggs, and quiches, while waiting to hear from Wintegreat. He does the strict minimum, retreats into his shell, and never gives a minute of overtime despite his managerial position. In no time, he's ruffled the feathers of the rest of the team, primarily the women, with whom he's bossy and sexist. Several of them complain to my mother, who discovers a new facet of Mohammad's personality. She can no longer deny he's not cut out for the job. His lack of consideration and absence of empathy comes across as selfishness. Marie-France can tell he's struggling. He no longer stops by to see her when he comes home. He increasingly declines her invitations to go to the movies. Once more, he withdraws into his own little world. She's taken in a 20-year-old man, put a roof over his head, fed him, found him a job, spent time with him, and grown attached to him. She placed a lot of hope in him, and now that she's given him new responsibilities and the opportunity to climb the ladder in the field, he falls short.

She summons him to voice her disappointment. "This position is an amazing opportunity for you. You don't realize how lucky you are to be managing a tea room in just a few weeks. Quite frankly, I feel you're behaving like a spoiled child."

He listens silently, waiting for her to finish raking him over the coals. Then he steps toward her with tears in his eyes. "I need a hug."

My mother gathers him in her arms for a long embrace. "Don't be mad at me," he pleads. "You're all I've got."

• • •

Mohammad is still waiting to hear if he's been selected for an interview, but he decides to start preparing, just in case. He watches Ted Talks on Youtube for inspiration, to see how people from around the world present and share their experiences in their given fields. He writes *One Ted Talk a day keeps the darkness away* on a piece of paper and posts it above his desk.

Later, during one of my trips to Paris, I notice the quote tacked to the wall in his room. I tell him how my daughter Philomene, shortly after we moved to New York when she was 17, was asked to give a Ted Talk about SpeciWomen, a website she'd created to promote young women artists. Mohammad is impressed. We sit down at his computer and watch my daughter, alone on stage before 300 people, address— in fluent English—the inequality of men and women in the art world.

It's us, girls and boys of today, who are building the world of tomorrow. It is us who have the power to make our future look like what we want it to look like. Because boys of our generation, for example, know the diversity of points of view is enriching, and how putting a blindfold on female perspective, which represents half of the world, limits the comprehension and the evolution of humanity in all fields. SpeciWomen is my little step to make my future, our future, equal and better. If everyone steps forward and gives a little bit of themselves, then things are going to happen really fast. And I, citizen of an Occidental country, where women and men possess equal rights, and for all the women who do not have these rights, I think it's a duty to show how powerful, confident, intelligent, ambitious, hard-working and fearless we are. And that we're not missing anything. Thank you.

As the audience applauds in the background, Mohammad turns to me, his eyes gleaming with admiration. He has every intention to be a full part of the future generation Philomene talks about. The one that is going to change the world.

For Christmas vacation, Mohammad goes to visit an Afghan friend in Switzerland. He met Morteza in Kabul during his rap years. Back then, he was a cameraman and directed music videos. Later, he made a documentary on a Taliban war leader in the north of Afghanistan. A few days after the shoot was over, the man was assassinated. Morteza knew he was in danger and fled. Mohammad was in Sri Lanka at the time and told his friend to come join him. He greeted Morteza with his wife and daughter at the Colombo airport, then housed them a few weeks in his tiny hotel room until they could get a visa for Europe.

Mohammad travels with a car-sharing service, the cheapest way to get to Switzerland. He spends the whole ride chatting with the three other passengers: a retired Parisian couple, and a student off to spend the holidays with her Swiss boyfriend.

When Mohammad arrives, he and Morteza embrace. They haven't seen each other since Colombo and are both moved to tears. They spend five days exploring the town, talking, laughing and cooking. What joy to speak in his native language with someone who shares the same background and gets him. On New Year's Eve, they stroll through the city until dawn, drinking beer and smoking cigarettes, enjoying the fireworks and enormous freedom.

For the trip back, Mohammad finds a cheap one-way plane ticket online. He lands in Roissy, and for the first time since he'd arrived in France two years earlier, he finds himself at customs. Nervously, he holds out his ID. The customs officer glances at his travel document and waves him through. He had no idea crossing a border could be so simple.

In the commuter train back to Paris, Mohammad thinks about the new period he's about to embark upon. 2017, the year of possibilities. He feels optimistic. Even if he's aware of the obstacles he still must overcome. He can tell the future is looking brighter. He's anxious to leave behind the solitude that's plagued him for years.

He simply must get into university. He'll be able to meet people there, make friends, and maybe even fall in love.

Things would be so different if he had a girlfriend. Someone he could share his joys and anxieties with. Someone he could lean on and who would lean on him. Someone he could cuddle, kiss and make love to. The thought makes his head spin. At 20, he's terribly frustrated, sexually speaking.

He brought it up once with my mother. He'd met a girl in a bar he liked. They went to a party then said goodbye outside her building. My mother encouraged Mohammad to call her, but he didn't dare. He was completely at a loss. He had no idea how to go about it. He couldn't communicate with her. He was afraid of not being as funny as in his native language, of not being mysterious, of seeming stupid. He felt like he had nothing to offer. Besides, he didn't want to risk failure. A broken heart, on top of everything else, would simply be too much. He knew he couldn't bear it.

So, he clings to the idea that, if one day he manages to get into a prestigious school, it will give him confidence, status and legitimacy. He'll feel more comfortable meeting other people, especially girls. He'll no longer be the refugee everyone pities and either takes under their wing or rejects. People will appreciate him once more for his intelligence, humor, uniqueness and the complexity of his personality.

Marguerite phones Mohammad to tell him he's been selected for an interview. She explains what to expect, reassures him it won't last long, and advises him to wear his best clothes.

He holes up in his room and spends the next two days meditating. He has no idea what lies ahead. All he knows is that they're looking for motivated people. He's going to try to be as natural as possible, talk about his passion for international politics, and clearly outline his project: getting into Sciences Po.

He thinks a lot, talks out loud, tries to imagine what questions they'll ask, practices his answers. He feels increasingly at ease. He's not going to let this opportunity slip away.

After 48 hours of solitude, he finally needs to share the news. He heads down the stone staircase and enters the living room. It's dark. My mother's not there. She doesn't answer her phone. He sits on the plush, almond-green velvet couch and dials Jawad's number. Even 5,000 miles away, he's still Mohammad's closest friend. Jawad congratulates him, but Mohammad can hear the weariness in his voice. The United Nations still hasn't given him an answer. How can he keep from losing his mind after three years hiding on a beach in Sri Lanka? No work, no rights, and nothing but fear, precarity and uncertainty for the future.

Mohammad hangs up, nestles back into the soft cushions and sits there a moment in the dark. He feels powerless. He wants to be able to help his friend, but he is already so busy trying to save his own skin every day.

He hears the front door open. The parquet in the foyer creaks. The light comes on. My mother appears. "What are you doing here in the dark?"

"Waiting for you. I heard back. I've gotten an interview for the preparatory class in two days."

"Wow! Congratulations, Mohammad!" She takes him into the kitchen, pulls a bottle of white wine from the fridge and pours them two glasses. "Here's to you!"

Mohammad beams at her and takes a long sip of cool wine. My mother studies him. He looks so confident, suddenly. Perhaps going to school isn't such a bad idea after all. She feels like one of those awkward parents who aren't sure how to act around their children. Should she offer to help or let him manage on his own?

"Do you want me to go with you to the interview?"

Mohammad's face lights up. "That'd be great."

She figures she'll treat him the way she treats her sons. She'll be there if he needs her but won't impose. He's too old for that.

If he gets into university, will he still live with her? It reminds her of the days my brothers and I left the family nest to pursue our lives. She remembers being torn between joy at seeing her children take flight, and anxiety at no longer being there to protect them.

"I'm going up to bed. I want to be in good shape for my final preparations." Mohammad polishes off his wine and stands up.

"You need a suit."

The next morning, my mother takes Mohammad to the men's clothing shops in Saint-Germain-des-Prés. Together they pick out a navy-blue two-piece suit.

"You look amazing."

• • •

On Saturday, January 7th, Mohammad gets up, puts on his suit, and drinks the coffee my mother has prepared for him. Then they set off for the interview.

At 11:15 am, Mohammad steps into another dimension. He and my mother enter the lobby of an impressive, late 19th-century building and walk down a majestic hallway where clusters of students talk. They join the other candidates seated on the wooden benches of the large library. My mother tries to glean information from the professors in the room. They reassure her. It will soon be Mohammad's turn. She wishes him luck and slips away.

He studies the people lined up next to him, thinking how only 20 of them will be chosen.

A half-hour later, he's called in.

Mohammad sits down across from three people. A young man, a bald man in his fifties with glasses, and an elderly woman. "Would you rather speak in French or English?" she asks.

"I'm more comfortable in English, if it's alright with you."

"That's fine."

"I have to admit I'm extremely nervous. It's taken a long time for me to get here. This interview is critical for the rest of my life and for the future of Afghanistan. I may stammer occasionally, and I apologize in advance."

The bald man reassures him. "Relax, it's going to be fine. We're here for you."

Mohammad takes a deep breath and starts reading notes from his computer. He describes his journey. "I'll give you the basic outline, but if you want to know more, there's a book about me coming out next year by the famous French publisher, Flammarion."

The three jury members exchange an amused look.

Mohammad gains confidence and starts speaking off the cuff. He talks about his passion for international politics and music. He explains that even if he never returns to rap again in the future, the hip-hop culture will remain rooted in him as a counterpoint or counterculture that helps him put things in perspective and question a certain vision of society. "I'm not sure of anything. I'm here to learn."

"You wrote in your questionnaire that you would like to enter Sciences Po, particularly the Le Havre campus which is geared toward Asia. Why not the Menton campus which focuses on the political, economic and social issues of the Mediterranean, the Middle East and the Gulf?"

"I have nothing against the Arab world, but I'm an atheist. I believe in science and learning. I'd like to go to Le Havre to study political relations with Asia, China, Japan, and South Korea. Arabic countries have oil, but Asian countries have knowledge. That's what I'm interested in."

The interview was supposed to last a half-hour, but they let him go after 15 minutes. Mohammad is disconcerted. Is that a good or bad sign?

"Can you tell me if I have any chance of getting in?"

"We'll let you know as soon as possible."

He thanks the jury and is about to leave when the young professor says "goodbye" in Dari.

"That's why I'd like to study alongside you; you all speak at least ten languages."

My mother comes home after a long day. The house is quiet. She heads upstairs and knocks on Mohammad's door. No answer. She knocks again. Silence. She opens the door. The room's empty. No sign of life. Her blood runs cold. She glances around the room for a note or letter, some kind of explanation. Nothing. She heads back downstairs. Searches the kitchen, living room, dining room. Still nothing. In the bathroom, she discovers her jewelry box empty. She sits down on the edge of the tub and starts to cry. Finally, she finds a letter Mohammad left on her desk, explaining how he had to leave unexpectedly. His mother and brother had just arrived in England and wanted him to come join them as soon as he could.

My mother wakes with a start. It's still dark out. She's never had this dream before.

Mohammad was supposed to stay with her a year; soon it will be 18 months. She's grown attached to him and doesn't want him to go. She knows he'll leave one day, but his college plans have speeded things up. His unassuming presence, their Sunday movie outings, their conversations in the kitchen over a glass of red, weekends in Recloses, their one-on-one dinners in neighborhood restaurants, his kindness... She remembers how on her birthday he gave her a bouquet of flowers that was "more than beautiful." He looked so elegant in a jacket and trousers cut "just the right length." He told her she was his guide, his fairy godmother. She loves talking to him. What will she do when he's no longer around? She knows there's no going back. The room won't stay empty. Will she lodge another young man? A woman? Children? A whole family? She'd rather not think about it yet and enjoy Mohammad's presence while she can.

As a young filmmaker, I was fortunate to be surrounded by great *cinephiles*, an endangered species. They were my mentors, and they inspired, advised, and supported me. François, Claude, Bruno, and Jean. Jeannot to his loved ones. I'd just learned of his death from Laurence, his wife, and a friend, and I decide to fly to Paris for the funeral.

We had lunch together just a month ago. He complained, as usual, grumbling about getting too old and growing increasingly tired, but he continued to watch several movies every day.

"I just saw *Nocturnal Animals*, the new Tom Ford. It's a killer. Trust your daddy! You can't miss this one. The opening credits alone are worth the price of admission."

A week later, he went into the hospital for some routine tests and never came out.

He and Laurence had come to visit us in New York the previous fall. Jean was like a kid, fascinated by the way people looked and dressed, the huge steaks, the colorful jars of Mexican peppers in grocery store windows, how late shops were open, the taste of local Brooklyn IPA, and our new life in general. We spent a lot of time screening films in our basement. He'd seen all the movies before, of course, but couldn't hide his pleasure at sharing them with us. One Friday afternoon, as we'd just begun watching a Lubitsch from the German period, both our cell phones rang at the same time. We immediately switched off the movie and turned on CNN, showing the first footage from the mass shootings at the Bataclan in Paris. We were stunned and frustrated not to be with our families during this tragedy, but glad we were together to mutually support each other.

I think of all this, as I walk through the damp, cold air on the parvis of the Pere-Lachaise cemetery in northern Paris, where my father was cremated six years earlier.

While I'm in Paris, I stop by the bank to work out a loan. Life in New York is proving more expensive than planned. The banker asks about my mother. We've known each other a long time; for years he's handled the family finances. I tell him about Mohammad's arrival in her life. He can't believe it. "Your mother's an amazing woman."

To hear him say it, you'd think she'd just saved Africa from famine or solved global warming. This man manages the largest fortunes in France, but this is the first time he's ever heard of one of his clients taking someone into their home.

As I leave, my phone vibrates in my jacket pocket. The screen says *Mohammad*. I answer.

"I got in!"

"That's great! When did you hear?"

"Just now. I got an email. Classes start next week, and in six months, I'll be able to take the entrance exam to Sciences Po."

"Did you tell my mother?"

"Of course. She's over the moon."

I suggest we celebrate right away and hop in a cab.

The driver has the radio on. Live coverage of Donald Trump's inauguration. It's too loud. The bits and pieces I hear make me sick.

• • •

Mohammad is waiting for me outside the restaurant, a touchstone of French cuisine. I give him a big hug, then we go in where its warm and sit on the red leather benches. We order. Farmhouse pâté, cheese soufflé and Chateaubriand pepper steak. We have things to celebrate, and things to forget.

"Today is the inauguration, isn't it?" he asks.

"Yep. He's going to take the oath at the Capital, then shake hands with Obama who'll fly off in a helicopter with Michelle. After that, Trump will be on his own in the White House. It's horrifying."

"Today is also the day I found out that I was accepted into a major university to prepare for Sciences Po." We clink glasses. "I've always wanted to go to school, study and learn, but I never had the chance. I want to meet as many professors and intellectuals as possible. I'm so hungry for knowledge. I want to rebuild myself by discovering who I am. And for the first time, I'm going to be able to focus on it 100%."

"It's funny to think how, like in a fantasy, we're now stuck with the worst. But you're entering Sciences Po. You're the future. Here, try the chutney with your pâté; it's delicious."

"Learning is the only thing that keeps me going. I know the next six months are crucial. I'm going to have to work my tail off. It's going to be tough, but if it were easy, everyone would do it."

"It's the biggest challenge of your life. Probably not the hardest, with everything you've been through, but no doubt the most exciting. I'm happy for you."

"Thanks. You know, there aren't that many people I can share things with, good or bad. I Skype with my friends and family, obviously, but it's not the same."

"Did you tell them?"

"My big sister cried."

"Did they know you'd had the interview?"

"Of course. Back in Kabul, I was always saying how I wanted to go to Sciences Po, but everyone thought I was crazy. There was no way it could ever happen."

"They know about Sciences Po back in Kabul?"

"You bet! It's like Oxford or Harvard. I dreamed about it every night for years. I have no choice; I have to get in."

"More wine?"

He nods. I fill his glass.

"It takes a lot of motivation, endurance and self-confidence. Plus, you need to meet the right people at the right time. That's something you must trigger, it doesn't just fall from the sky. I can't tell you how many times I almost threw in the towel. It's people like your mother who gave me the strength to keep going."

"Hold on, you're not there yet. You're going to have to work like hell to pass the entrance exam."

"I know. But this is already a huge step forward."

We raise our glasses in another toast.

"Where do you see yourself in ten years?"

"Well, I figure I will have studied at several major universities, in France and abroad. I'll have a lot of knowledge about society, politics and sociology. Then I'll go back to Afghanistan. I want to help the people there. His voice lowers. He tells me how he plans to work undercover. He wants to get as close as he can to the power, to change people's thinking without the authorities noticing. He needs to find a way to sow the seeds of doubt in the minds of young people. So they'll stop swallowing everything they're told, condemning them to a life of ignorance or else death. He wants to go back and break into the circle of leaders. He dreams of getting into the Ministry of Education where he'll have access to school textbooks. That's where he needs to focus. Surreptitiously changing the content of schoolbooks. It's crucial for kids to learn from an early age to think differently; to not blindly follow obscure precepts without asking questions. "I'll probably die before I can see the results of what I hope to do. But at least I'll go in peace."

"The religious authorities will never let you do that."

"I'll have to be very careful. Obviously, I'll pretend to be a good Muslim. I'll never let on I'm an atheist, I'm no fool. For now, it's just a vision, a utopia. I don't have a plan yet. But if you go back there holding degrees, the government needs you. So few people have an education. Most of the country's rulers are war chiefs. Leadership was given to them because of their victories, not because a political program or vision for their country. You have to know the right people. For instance, I'm Hazara; some members of government are from the same ethnic group. They're the ones I'll go see. There's a shortage of people like me. Someone has to do something about it."

He pauses to sip from his fourth glass of wine. He's on a roll now, as if he's giving a sermon. "The upcoming generation needs to learn to question the existence of God. They're completely blocked by religion, they can't do anything, they can't think, their brains and hearts are locked up by propaganda. I know because for a long time, I was like them. Someone needs to explain that God doesn't control our lives, we control our lives. Once they've understood that, they can practice any religion they want, but at least they'll have had the choice."

With each successive glass of wine, we clink glasses and toast "to the future!" It's the mantra we've shared since the first time we ever drank together.

"Education is the only thing that can save the world. Most wars are led by ignorant people. When there are wars, there's no security; without security, no money; without money, no education; and without education, there are more wars. It's a vicious circle. When your only goal in life is survival, education becomes a luxury, not a priority." He shrugs. "Luckily there are people like your mother. I'm going to try my hardest to pass on the love she gave me."

"You've got your whole life ahead of you."

The waiter brings *crêpes Suzette* and performs the flambé before us. My gaze meets Mohammad's. His eyes gleam from alcohol, and in them I recognize the joy of sharing this moment. Above all, pride at how far he's come.

Six months later.

It's summer. After a few weeks in Europe, I'm about to return home to Brooklyn. I sit alone in the kitchen eating my toast. The radio is on. A journalist announces in a monotone that a ship funded by European extreme right parties is sailing around the Mediterranean to repel the migrant boats trying to reach the Italian coasts.

My mother comes in and sits across from me. She pours herself a cup of tea.

"What time are you picking up the van?"

Tuesday, August 22, is a special day. Mohammad is leaving the house. He got accepted into Sciences Po and is moving to the Le Havre campus.

About 20 candidates were chosen by Wintegreat. Each of them was assigned a coach and a mentor to steer their project. At a cocktail party, Mohammad was introduced to David and Antoine, the team who would help him write his resume, fill out applications, choose his field, practice for interviews, etc. David was a Sciences Po alumnus who volunteered as an homage for France welcoming his father from Morocco in the 1950s. To show that this sort of generosity was still possible. Antoine, from a wealthy family, was in his final year at the ESCP business school. He had been woken to the plight of migrants by some friends and wanted to help. It didn't take long for them to realize Mohammad had a great deal of potential, so they stepped up the process. For six months, they met several times a week to hammer out the most effective strategy.

To celebrate getting in, Mohammad asked my mother to organize a dinner at her home to thank all the people who'd helped him since he arrived in France.

Everyone gathered around a large table out in the yard. There was Catherine, the volunteer from Singa; Sylvie, the restaurant manager from Merci; Laurence, the dentist friend; Bernard, the producer/French teacher; my Aunt Martine; Marguerite, his contact at Wintegreat; Antoine, his coach; David, his mentor; Marie-Hélène, who ironed his shirts for a year-and-a-half; and her daughter Jessica who worked with him at Miss Marple. Mohammad took a group photo and sent it to the two Marcs, his guardian angels from Colombo and Sarrebourg. It was moving to see all these people from different backgrounds, most of whom had never met before that night. They all gathered to celebrate a young man who was sleeping in the streets a year and a half ago. Now, thanks to their solidarity, he was about to enter one of the most prestigious schools in the world.

Mohammad joins us in the kitchen and makes himself a cup of coffee. "The day they announced the results, I wore the suit you bought me. People were impressed. The director of the school told us there were future presidents and ministers among us. It was amazing!"

My mother applauds him.

"This is my last breakfast in this house. I entered here a dead man; now I'm leaving alive."

"You can come back whenever you like. When my children left home, they kept their rooms. It's the same for you."

It's the first time I hear her address him like her own son.

After breakfast, Adeeb, an Afghan friend who worked with Mohammad in the army, shows up to help. As they start gathering Mohammad's things in the foyer, I go pick up the van at the rental agency. The last time I did this was a year ago when my daughter left for college. I figured the next time will be my son. Last year, there were only a few bags of clothes, boxes of books, and a shelf. This time, it's an actual move. A couch, two armchairs, a bed, a fridge, a TV, etc. Originally, we'd looked for a furnished studio apartment. We spent an entire day, phoning different real estate agents in Le Havre. With a 450€-a-month budget, the apartments available ranged from 200 to 270 square feet. I explained on the phone it was for a student at Sciences Po, and that my mother would stand as guarantor. Everyone I spoke to was charming and eager to please, until I mentioned Mohammad's name. Their tone changed. "You know, there are lots of viewings. It'll probably be rented out by then."

As a privileged white male, I'd never been exposed to such blatant racism.

Finally, we managed to set up five apartment viewings for the following week. Since I was away at the time, my mother made the trip with Mohammad, aware that the owners would react differently if she was at his side. She carefully selected an outfit for the occasion and put on her Gucci mules.

Almost immediately, she declared the studios we had selected as "too small, too dark, and too depressing." Instead, she set her sights on a "wonderful little building" just a stone's throw from campus. A 540 square foot apartment was going for just a little bit more than what we'd been looking at. The only hitch: it was unfurnished. She offered to pay the 50€-a-month difference and provide the furniture. Mohammad didn't need to be asked twice. In the wave of a magic wand, he went from a studio with sofa bed, to an elegantly laid out two-room apartment. Our initial plan to toss a couple suitcases in the trunk of my father's car and hit the road to Normandy, just the three of us, was no longer in the cards. We needed to organize a real move, complete with help.

My son, Aurelio, arrives and starts loading the furniture with Mohammad and Adeeb. My mother, who woke up with a fever and a raging sorethroat, does a steam-inhalation in the kitchen while waiting to go. Once the van is packed to the gills, Mohammad climbs in the front seat between me and my mother, and we set out for Le Havre. While stopped at a red light before getting on the highway, a man with an olive complexion comes up to the van. He holds a cardboard sign scrawled *Syrian Family*. I fish around in my pocket and hand him some coins. When the light turns green, I catch Mohammad's gaze.

"That man is me. Every time I meet someone like him, I see myself. I never asked for handouts, but I was in the street. I know exactly how they feel. The hunger, the fear, the humiliation and despair."

We get on the highway. My mother dozes with her head against the window. I turn to Mohammad. "What did you think the first time I asked you to tell me your story?"

"Honestly? I can't lie because you're my friend now. But at the time, I thought you were full of shit: like everybody else who'd promised me something in the past. I figured it would lead nowhere. 'My mom's refugee is exotic; he'd make a good story.' Then boom, you'd get some better idea and forget all about me. That's what I thought. Most of the people who offered to help weren't really thinking about me, they were thinking about their connection to your mother. They wanted to help 'Marie-France's migrant.' I still have trouble trusting anyone. I still need time to put all the puzzle pieces back together. So, I didn't want to put too much stock in it. Even if you were Marie-France's son, and she was the only person I could rely on at the time. But now there are two of you."

We drive along in silence. We pass Poissy, Mantes-la-Jolie, Rouen, Honfleur. Mohammad stares out the window at the horizon. He smiles, as he reminds me of a passage from the book that changed his life: *By no means are you condemned to this kind of life. You can pursue a higher education in any field that you want, at the best universities in the world*. That was a century ago.

I park the van outside the "wonderful little building." We start unloading the boxes, while my mother signs the lease. The owner keeps stealing glances to make sure we aren't nicking the freshly-painted walls in the stairway. We lug everything up to the third floor. The woman, accustomed to student tenants, looks quite surprised by the quality of the furniture. We fill the two spacious, sun-drenched rooms with a brown velvet couch, antique paintings, brass lamps with Art Deco lampshades, a giant flat-screen TV, and an oriental rug. She seems both intrigued and reassured. Once all the forms are signed, she hands Mohammad the key, and slips away. I spend the next hour getting the gas, water, and electricity turned on, while my mother hangs paintings with her tape measure. Can't leave anything to chance.

Mohammad tries to give his opinion on where things should go, but my mother won't hear of it. "Let Mom handle this." I catch Adeeb's amused gaze. Since the day began, he's looked stunned by the whole show he's been a spectator to. From the first act in the *hôtel particulier* at the Invalides, to the final scene in this roomy apartment in the middle of Le Havre. From the luxurious set of furniture, he helped transport, to the role of my mother, the lead actress, both controlling and protective. It's a culture shock for the young man who's lived alone in a tiny studio in a working class neighborhood since he came to Paris.

Once the final details are settled, my mother plops on the couch to admire her handiwork. She's lent him a part of her life, passed on her good French taste, set him up like her own son. The apartment looks like that of an heir from a fine family. "You're going to be the star of the campus."

Mohammad is delighted.

It's time to go. We all hug tightly. As we drive away, I spot tears in the corner of Mohammad's eye as he waves goodbye.

I suggest to my mother we grab some seafood before heading back to Paris. She's thrilled, despite her cold, and guides me along the Normandy roads to the port of Trouville-sur-Mer.

We get a table on the terrace, order a dozen oysters, and a bottle of white. It's starting to cool down a little.

"In the end, Mohammad was the only one who made it into a prestigious university. Good thing he happened along."

Neither I, the filmmaker, nor Julien with his multitude of trendy restaurants, nor Thomas with his successful children's clothing brand, pursued this kind of education.

My mother, moved, shrugs and smiles. We raise our glasses to Mohamad's future.

A few days later, I send Mohammad an email to check in. How does he like his new apartment? Is the electricity and water working? How was his first day of school?

He replies:

> *Benoit,*
> *I can't believe all this is real. I can't stop patting myself on the back.*
> *Yesterday, the professors and campus staff introduced themselves and told us to give it the best*

*we've got. The director of the school ended his
speech with, "Work hard, but don't forget to have
fun." I was all choked up. I didn't know such a place
could exist. Then we went to Etretat. It was amazing.
We watched the sun set over the cliffs, and drank
till all hours.*

*It's so hard to get into this school, I feel like I'm
surrounded by geniuses. What am I doing here?
Cheers,
Med.*

EPILOGUE

The family is gathered in the living room. A fire crackles and candles are burning. The coffee table is draped with a red tablecloth, loaded with glasses of champagne, canapes of foie gras, taramasalata, and grilled almonds. A mountain of gifts is piled beneath a 10-foot Christmas tree festooned with lights and garlands. The children are impatient and rip open their gifts two at a time. Med receives a black wool turtleneck sweater, a shirt with a mandarin collar, leather gloves and a baseball cap stamped *Paris* in white. He smiles, thanks everyone and apologizes; he didn't buy any presents, he didn't know. It's his first Christmas.

His exams ended the day before. He hurried back to Paris and settled into the upstairs room for the vacation. Eleonore and I needed a backup plan in a neighborhood hotel. It's kind of fun to play tourist in your own city.

He tells me about Sciences Po. Most of the other students have years of studies under their belts, while Med spent his childhood learning the Koran, leaving school at 15. He has no diploma nor any of the work methods his classmates developed in their preparatory classes. They're assigned several hundred pages of reading each day, expected to analyze it all in written essays. At first, he had absolutely no clue where to begin. And for fear of being marginalized, Med tried to hide his shortcomings from the others. His first grades were disastrous, and he was filled with self-doubt. He wanted to throw in the towel. When he came back to Paris for the fall break, he discussed it with my mother. She bucked him up and urged him to tell his teachers, to quit hiding his past, and own up to his weaknesses. So what, if the other students no longer consider him an equal? He can make up for that later. As soon as he went back, he made an appointment with the director of the school who promised to give him special attention. Med felt less alone, and his motivation came back.

It's been a year since I've known Med. I'm not talking about the handful of times we bumped into each other in my mother's house, but from the moment where he decided to share his story with me. A story he'd never told anyone before, which will now be known to the world. A story that echoes my own conquest of the West and gave me a better understanding of how a person can reinvent themselves by getting distance from their family. A story that has made the two of us friends. An unsung story of the woman who spent two years at his side. I met him thanks to my mother. Now it's my turn to introduce him to her.

It's raining outside. I sit in the back of a café near the Bastille. A curt, nervous bartender is arguing with an olive-skinned man with black hair wearing a blue apron. I hear the bartender snap, "How does it feel to spend your life peeling potatoes and cleaning other people's shit?" The man slinks back into the kitchen, without a word. I think of Med and all the political refugees, exiles, undocumented immigrants, stateless people and migrants with nowhere to go. The thousands of human beings who are chased out, stigmatized, exploited, enslaved, ransomed or rejected, who didn't have his luck, his strength or his intelligence.

Tomorrow, I'll fly back home across the Atlantic. Soon it will be the first anniversary of Donald Trump taking office. Time has gone by, but the wound hasn't healed. Every day brings a new amendment, more provocation, another tweet, a fresh incitement to hate. The megalomaniac billionaire is systematically dismantling the U.S., while the whole world looks on in horror. Before I left New York last month, I attended a conference with Jodie Foster on the role of women in Hollywood. Someone asked how she felt about the new president. She replied, "To keep from crying, I think of my daughter who's learning how to resist." It's the only way to hold despair at bay. Resist. Everyone on their own level. That's exactly how I felt that first morning in November when, after receiving the electoral jolt, I found myself seated in the kitchen with my mother and Mohammad.

ASSOCIATIONS

SINGA
A citizen movement that creates opportunities for refugees and their host communities to meet and cooperate *www.singafrance.com*

WINTEGREAT
A program that breathes new life into refugees' professional projects *www.wintegreat.org*

MERCI FOUNDATION
Created to help children throughout the world and finance acts of humanitarian development, particularly in the fields of health, education and culture *www.merci-merci.com/en/fonds-dotation*

ACKNOWLEDGEMENTS

Eléonore, for her ever-precious advice,

Alix, for her continued trust,

Julie, for her eagle eye,

as well as
Marie-France, Mohammad, Catherine, Richard, Guillaume, David, Antoine, Marguerite, Théo, Philomène, Alban, François, Bruno, both Juliens, Thomas, Jean, Thibault, Nathalie, Soizic, Florence, Laure and Tatiana.

And, also for the English-language version, Suzanne, Kelly, Frederico, Dominick, Michelle and Robbie.

—Benoit Cohen, New York, May 2019

BIOGRAPHY

Born in 1969, **Benoit Cohen** is a French producer, filmmaker, and screenwriter. After studying architecture in Paris, he attended New York University and studied filmmaking. When he came back to France, he started his own production company, Shadows Films. After producing several short films, he directed his first feature film *Caméléone* in 1996.

Between 2000 and 2014, Cohen produced and directed five other feature films (including *Our Precious Children* and *If You Love Me Follow Me*), a few documentaries and three TV Series. His last movie, *You'll Be a Man* was a significant success at film festivals around the United States (selected for more than 60 festivals and won 40 awards).

In 2014, after moving to Brooklyn, Cohen drove a taxi cab around the five boroughs, for several months, to gain perspective for a screenplay about a French actress becoming a taxi driver in New York. He wrote *Yellow Cab*, a book about this experience, which was published in May 2017 by Pointed Leaf Press. A movie adaptation is scheduled to be shot in the spring of 2020.

Mohammad, My Mother & Me, is his second book be published in the United States.

PUBLISHER/EDITORIAL DIRECTOR Suzanne Slesin
CREATIVE DIRECTOR Frederico Farina
MANAGING EDITOR Kelly Koester
DESIGNER Dominick Santise Jr.

ISBN: 978-1-938461-85-9
Library of Congress Number: 2019940253
First Edition 10 9 8 7 6 5 4 3 2 1
Printed in China

Original French edition of
Mohammad, ma mère et moi © Flammarion, Paris, 2018

Pointed Leaf Press, LLC.
136 Baxter Street, Suite 1C, New York, NY 10013
www.pointedleafpress.com